Bronze Shields:
A Black Police Organization's Fight for Equality and Justice in Newark, NJ
(An Oral History)

Marcus Reeves

with James Du Bose

Copyright © 2021 Romarc Media

All rights reserved.

ISBN: 9798525301887

DEDICATION

To my wife, Ronke Idowu Reeves, for helping me find the path to this story, and to my son, Monroe Olusegun Babatude Reeves…
(Marcus Reeves)

To my wife, Alice, for her words of encouragement…
(James Du Bose)

	Introduction	i
1	Seven Steps Toward Justice (1959-1965)	1
2	Standing on the Verge (1966-1969)	23
3	Guardians of Change (1970-1972)	42
4	Bronze Rising (1972-1981)	63
5	Changing Shields (1982-1998)	86
6	Newark's New Breed (1999-2008)	141
7	Bronze and Beyond	172
	Acknowledgments	183
	About the Authors	184
	Bronze Shields Griots	185

Introduction

This story of the Bronze Shields comes at a crucial time in America. A national push for major police reform, following the murder of George Floyd, marks a milestone within Black America's long-time struggle against abusive and racist police. But there's also been a long-time struggle for justice inside police departments nationwide for Black officers. And if there was a word that conjured the birth of the Bronze Shields in 1959 it was "justice." That's because this New Jersey-based African American police association was born out of its absence. Founded during the dawn of the civil rights movement, the Bronze Shields was the vision of officers like Floyd Bostic Jr., Edward Williams, and Horace Braswell who felt a need for solidarity in the face of discrimination, racial hostility, and white supremacy within the Newark Police Department. "We'd get together, have lunch, and discuss things about the police department that were wrong and should be changed," explained Horace Braswell. "Among those things included how Black police officers were treated."

Before the Bronze Shields, there was a movement of Black police associations dating back to the formation of the Texas Negro Peace Officers' Association in 1935. Organizations like this one as well as the Texas and Oklahoma Association of Negro Peace Officers (founded in 1937) and the Miami Colored Police Benevolent Association (formed in 1944) were formed to combat on-the-job racism many Black officers dealt with in the South. But this issue wasn't just a problem for cops below the Mason Dixon Line or in middle America. For Black officers in Newark's 1956 police recruitment class—the largest group of Black recruits at that time—racial segregation was an unspoken part of the job. In addition to Blacks being outright discouraged from joining the Newark Police Department, those who joined the force soon discovered they couldn't ride in police cars or on police motorcycles or be partnered with white officers (among other restrictions). The Bronze Shields developed as a means of fighting for the rights of Black police officers. What the organization would eventually do over six decades was help change the face, complexion and gender of the Newark Police Department and its leadership. They also helped foster a healthier relationship between the police and Newark's Black and brown communities. This is the story of the Bronze Shields's journey toward equality and justice, a 60-year tale of the organization's trek toward a more equitable future as a civil rights organization, a de facto union, a social club, community advocates, and a voice for the voiceless. It's an evolutionary story of resistance and struggle, of camaraderie and internal strife, of losses and historic triumphs.

Just as the organization's history is intrinsic to Newark's transformation into a chocolate city, this is also a story of the Bronze Shield's birthplace. Much of this oral history is told within the context of events—from white flight in the 1950s to the 1967 riots to the election of Newark's first Black mayor and beyond—which caused Newark's racial and political transformation. That's because the Bronze Shields and its members both witnessed and participated in these moments. Likewise, these events helped foster the impact of the Bronze Shields had on New Jersey's largest city. Like many predominately-Black urban centers across America, Newark—once vilified—is now on the verge of an economic and cultural renaissance. In other words, it's going through gentrification. Also important to this story is the Bronze Shields's mission of aiding the community, a tenet that has provided perhaps the strongest bond between police and Newark's mostly Black and Latino residents. The Bronze Shields helped build this union through charity and mentorship as well as offering compassion in times of crisis. "During the 1967 rebellion people asked for the Bronze Shields," said former Bronze Shields president Levi A, Holmes II. "They didn't want to talk to an officer unless he was a Bronze Shields." At a time when the media is filled with the tension between police officers and America's Black communities, the Bronze Shields's tale is an example of the affirmative outcome compassion from law enforcement can have on this often frayed relationship. Over the years, there have been a couple of attempts to tell the Bronze Shields story. Along with an unfinished history manuscript written by James Du Bose, Floyd Bostic Jr. helped produce a short documentary. Finally came the format I thought would best tell this tale: an oral history told by a cross-section of members and associates. The 30-plus interviews done for this book thoroughly encapsulate what the Bronze Shields fought for and what they've accomplished. Another important revelation this history illuminates is what the organization has meant to the city of Newark and what it has achieved for its residents.

Chapter 1

SEVEN STEPS TOWARD JUSTICE

(1959-1965)

Where many ethnic-based police unions and associations were created as social/professional networks for officers who share an ethnic and cultural background, the Bronze Shields sprang from a painfully inevitable aspect of African American life: facing racism and white supremacy. No discussion about the Bronze Shields or its genesis can be had without an examination of the racial dynamic of its birthplace, Newark, N.J. Since its founding in 1666, New Jersey's largest city had become one of America's bustling industrial urban centers and home to a myriad of working-class European communities—foreign and native-born Irish, German, Jewish and Italian. With its huge manufacturing base, Newark gained much of its growing African American population via the great migration—from the 1920s to 1960s—of southern Blacks moving north in search of better jobs, housing and opportunities, and less Jim Crow. A long-standing joke amongst many Black residents was that they'd settled in the city by mistake, having confused Newark with New

York. Unfortunately Black residents discovered—like numerous African Americans moving to cities all over America—they'd escaped legal segregation in the south only to find de facto racism in the north. This racial caste system was upheld and maintained by whites whose families arrived in America at the dawn of the 20th century. While no "Whites Only" signs blocked Black people's entrance into upward mobility, what replaced them was a silent, but keen understanding of where Blacks were allowed and not allowed to go within the city limits.

James Du Bose, Bronze Shields, NPD (1956-1985): Edward Williams, who would become Newark's first black police captain, told me a story about he and his brother Leroy as youngsters. They went to a public pool in Newark's Fourth Ward, now known as the Central Ward. When Edward and his brother attempted to pay the ten cents for admission they were told by a white attendant at the desk, "No niggers allowed in here except on Fridays." Edward said he and his brother looked at each other with deep sadness. They then turned around and walked home. While heading home they each wondered why the color of their skin prevented them from enjoying a pool. I can also remember black children learning how to swim in the Passaic River, which was filthy with industrial waste. For a lot of us, that was the only option since we weren't allowed in community pools on certain days. My uncle, who was 11 years old at the time, decided to go swimming in the river one day and nearly lost his life.

Leonard McGhee, Bronze Shields, NPD (1963-1989): You had certain sections of the city Blacks didn't live in or go into.

Junius Williams, Newark, N.J. Historian, Attorney: Black people could not walk on one side of Bloomfield Avenue—the Italians would kick your ass. It wasn't the south with Jim Crow, but it was just as bad for many reasons. Although you could go to places like the movies and the skating rink it wasn't that long since they'd been desegregated.

Harold Gibson, Bronze Shields, NPD (1961-1985): The East Ward up to downtown was mostly whites—Polish and Italians. In the West Ward, that was primarily Irish. The Central Ward was the Black section. You couldn't buy or rent a place in the other areas. Few blacks lived in the other parts. There was a place called Olympic Park that was frequented by mostly Jewish people. Very rarely did Black people go there. It was a public park, but you just didn't go there. As a Black person, you risked getting involved in a confrontation with the people who lived there.

Louis Greenleaf, Bronze Shields, NPD (1968-1994): It was like every other town back then. There were places you couldn't go. That's the way it was. We all lived in the Central Ward, and as you grew up in Newark, you began to know you couldn't go to certain neighborhoods. People didn't come out and say it. It was just there and hidden. At certain restaurants you couldn't go in the front door. You had to use the back door. One was a famous Jewish deli where we had to use the back door to get our sandwiches. Many of the downtown restaurants were like that too.

James Du Bose: The riots of 1967 are well known, but few people know of a mini-riot that occurred in the 1940s. Like the one in '67, the 1940's disturbance happened in the summer. It happened when a white police officer beat a Black woman on Springfield Avenue, which ran through the heart of the Central Ward. The community had already complained about several incidents of police brutality by white officers. Only this time, when nothing was done about it, the people began to show their anger. Stores were looted and fires were set. People wreaked havoc in the Central Ward.

Charles Knox: Bronze Shields, NPD (1965-1990): Growing up, I played sports. If you crossed Orange Street, which separated the North Ward from the Central Ward, and you went into the North Ward there was trouble. We went there to play baseball against the Italians. When we were done, we'd have to run out of there after the game was over. Otherwise they would beat you with baseball bats. But that's how it was in the 1940s and '50s. Everybody knew where their boundaries were. At the same time, there were efforts on the part of some involved in Newark politics who tried to create a climate of integration.

Thomas Murray, Bronze Shields, NPD (1963-1972): I've lived in Newark for years. Since I was in high school. I graduated in 1956. But I originally lived in Ohio. I had no problems as far as racism while living in Newark. I never experienced any racial things. I did experience racism while on the police force.

By the mid-1950s Newark's population was influx as thousands of upper and middleclass white residents began moving to the surrounding suburbs. The decade would also mark the start of the city's deindustrialization as factories and manufacturers began closing or moving out of Newark. The steady flow of African Americans, who were mostly relegated to the Central Ward, began moving to once mostly-white neighborhoods like South Ward's Clinton Hill and Vailsburg on the city's west side. Another agency to also feel this shift was the Newark Police Department, which had over 30 Black officers among its 1956 recruitment class. It was the largest group of African Americans hired in the department at the time. While the face of the police ranks began to change the power dynamics of race within the police department had not. The new Black recruits were soon made aware of how racism affected their place within the force.

James Du Bose: Black officers, at one time, were only able to arrest Blacks, not Caucasians.

Louis Greenleaf: We couldn't work in the North Ward, which was mostly Italian. You didn't get assigned there.

Thomas Murray: You had some white Newark police officers who resented Black police officers. I experienced that on Bergen Street. I was calling off duty and a white officer was about to call on duty. He came up behind me and put a pistol to the back of my head. When I got down to the precinct I told what he did and reported him. His response was, "I didn't know he was a cop." How in the hell he didn't know when I was in full uniform.

Charles Harris, Bronze Shields, NPD (1955-1984): Originally, I was assigned to nights, walking the night beat on Frelinghuysen Avenue. I walked that beat for at least two years. And I felt that I had enough experience to get into a radio car. But during that time we had Jim Crow in Newark. They wouldn't allow a Black police officer and a white to ride together. So, as a result, no Black man got into a radio car. We had to walk. We couldn't do traffic. We couldn't ride the motorcycles. The only job open to us was the night patrol. And then there were other experiences. When I made an arrest and made out an arrest sheet for a Black man, they always described a Black man as having maroon eyes. And I questioned that. But I couldn't get an answer from my lieutenant. They just thought it to be customary. Also, when a Black man was arrested the white policemen would always assault him right in the jail. But if you spoke up about it you got retaliation, like the worst assignment you could get.

Horace Braswell, Bronze Shields, NPD (1955-1984): I came on the Newark Police Department in June 1955. My first assignment was at the old 6th Precinct at Bigelow and Huntington. It was later changed to the 5th Precinct. I encountered my first experience of Jim Crow there. I couldn't ride in the radio car, and I was relegated to the night patrol. I did night patrol at the 5th Precinct for 18 months on Frelinghuysen Avenue. This area was located around the old projects on Ludlow Street. The department kept us—two other Black police officers, Charlie Harris, Freddie Cole and I— down there, out of the mainstream.

Floyd Bostic Jr., Bronze Shields, NPD (1956-1984): I was initially impressed that the Newark Police Department consisted of white police officers and a few Blacks. But there was no equality. I found that the conditions were very bad. While listening to roll call, you'd hear several of the lieutenants, when giving assignments, make racial remarks like, "Go up on Belmont Avenue and issue summonses to those coons." I remember after Horace Braswell and I heard a similar remark during roll call, we immediately approached the lieutenant. We said that it wasn't proper of him to make those kinds of remarks. Well, he didn't like the idea of us approaching him. But he had no choice but to admit he was wrong.

Janet Bostic, daughter of Floyd Bostic Jr.: The Black officers were always walking beats in isolated areas and dangerous neighborhoods. They were dropped off at Doremus Avenue, and they would have to walk down there with all the swamplands around them. My father told me a story of walking his beat downtown when his sergeant pulled up in a patrol car and called him over. It was pouring rain. My father was standing there, and they had the car window halfway down talking to him. They weren't really saying anything to him, just having a bullshit conversation. But my father noticed the driver was snickering. So he realized they were just screwing with him by having him out in the rain. He just walked away. He just went back to walking, even though the guy said, "I'm not done talking to you." My father said, "Well, I'm done talking to you."

Young Black recruits who joined the Newark Police Department in the 1950s were fueled with the intolerance for racism and inequality that was in lock step with a revolution reshaping America's social, racial and political landscape. A little over 200 miles south of Newark, in Washington D.C., Thurgood Marshall helped strike down school segregation with his Brown vs. Board of Education win in 1954. The civil rights movement, which ignited via the Montgomery Bus Boycott in 1955, began the work of challenging legal segregation and racial injustice. Such developments weren't lost on Newark police officers like Horace Braswell and Floyd Bostic Jr. who were among the new Black police recruits. While the two were well aware of the dilemma they faced—the biggest being the discrimination on the job—the main question was how were they going to deal with it.

James Du Bose: Many of the guys I came in with eventually decided to voice their concerns. We had to. I mean, when we reported to headquarters for the final health examination and interview, white detectives made wagers about how many of us wouldn't graduate from the police academy. I was among the 36 police recruits who graduated from the Newark police academy the following year in 1957. That graduating class was immediately distributed throughout the city's five precinct's foot patrol units. We were assigned the 4 p.m. to midnight and midnight to 8 am shifts. We weren't pleased with the hours, but at least we had hours. Most of the white officers hated having an integrated police department but they had no choice.

Floyd Bostic Jr.: There were times when police cars sat idle rather than team a Black and a white officer together. Incidents like that and other situations inspired me, Horace Braswell, Charles Harris and others to try and do something about this. At the time, there was another Black police organization called the Batons. But this was an organization strictly for social purposes. They'd give a dance and draw a big crowd once a year, and that was a success as far as they were concerned. But once the dance was over they weren't active until the next year. Then they'd give another affair. We went to some of the members of the Batons and we talked to them about the conditions we were experiencing in the police department. We asked some of the older members for their advice. Of course they sympathized with the problems we were having, but there was nothing else they could offer. I suspected there was nothing else they really wanted to do. They lowered their expectations to just accept the status quo.

Louis Greenleaf: The Batons didn't just represent Newark police officers they represented Essex County. They included men from the Sheriff's Department, from corrections and other departments.

A lot of the Batons would later become members of the Bronze Shields.

Harold Gibson: The Batons were, in my opinion, a different organization. They wanted to be a part of the department so badly that they followed whatever the white officers made them do. I don't want to be harsh, but that's my opinion.

Horace Braswell: When I became a motorcycle cop I was lucky enough to be paired with Floyd Bostic. We rode together constantly. Later, Charles Harris was moved to the motorcycle squad. Every day we all rode together. We'd get together, have lunch and discuss things we felt were wrong with the police department. Among those things included how the Black police officers were treated. We had nobody to fight for us and represent us. After talking about it daily, we decided to do something for ourselves. This became the idea of forming a club for Black police officers.

Floyd Bostic Jr.: Charlie Harris, Braswell and I decided to form an organization between us. It was an organization that would consist of other police officers that experienced discrimination and bigotry and knew they were being mistreated. So we began to meet regularly.

James Du Bose: We started meeting in the spring of 1958. I was recruited by a relative of mine who was a patrolman named William Millar. Then I recruited both of his partners, Patrolmen Norman Harris and Donald Harper. Neither had prior experience with forming an organization, except William. He was a former member of the Batons. So his experience was very much needed. Sunday meetings consisted of ideas on what we could do and how we could do things that would contribute towards a better Newark for the community and a better police department. At one Sunday meeting, all of the members agreed that it was time to appoint the organization's first president. The position was offered to William, but he refused because he'd just quit the Batons and didn't want it to appear he was forming a rival organization. But William did accept the position of parliamentarian. After talking it over, we all agreed the only other candidate who could handle the presidency was Floyd Bostic Jr. because it was his idea to unite Black officers. Floyd accepted the position and he was our first president.

Harold Gibson: As a leader, Floyd was very good at how he represented police officers on the force. He was one of the first Black officers to ride a motorcycle. His uniform was always clean. He was well polished with his shiny boots. His was an image of a police officer. He was the one you wanted to be like.

Floyd Bostic Jr.: Our first meeting was held at the Boys Club on High Street and West Kinney. We met there for several weeks until we got enough members to officially start an organization. Afterward we left the Boys Club and started meeting at my house on South 17th Street. We continued to hold meetings until we decided that we were going to form the Bronze Shields. Once the organization was formed we retained Paul Parker as an attorney to draw up a charter for us. We became a chartered organization in 1959. The founding members were me, Edwards Williams, William A. Stewart, Horace Braswell, Theodore Howard, Alfred Harris and Charles Harris. I was elected the first president and held that office for two terms.

James Du Bose: The Bronze Shields's name was adopted at the Boys Club. We selected it from a pool of suggested names. One name that was proposed was the Silver Shields. That got rejected because members said the word "silver" might be associated with the word white. The next name discussed was Black Shields. That was rejected because the word "black" at the time was considered derogatory. I suggested the name be the Bronze Shields. That one seemed more acceptable. It was voted upon and accepted as the name. Then a charter was eventually obtained for the Bronze Shields, Inc. as a non-profit and benevolent association of Black police officers of the Newark Police Department. The charter was obtained on February 21, 1959.

Horace Braswell: During one meeting, one of the things decided was the name. I don't remember who came up with it, but it was an appropriate name. It stuck.

James Du Bose: While we were putting the organization together, which we'd been doing privately, our plans to organize was leaked. Word had gotten to the police department that we were forming a Black policeman association. The department heads told us there was no need for an organization of our own because we had the Police Benevolence Association (P.B.A.). Of course, The Bronze Shields rejected the idea and stated that the P.B.A. was a bargaining agent. Besides, other ethnic groups had their own fraternal organizations. The German officers had the Steuben Society. The Italian officers had the Columbians. The Polish officers had the Falcons. The Jewish officers had the Shomrims. And the Irish officers had the Emeralds. The department heads begged to differ and accused us of being communist-inspired. Instead of scaring us, accusations like that only inspired us to keep going.

Harold Gibson: I think, initially, the Bronze Shields were also frowned upon by the other Black police officers, like the Batons, because it was well known that members of the Bronze Shields wanted to move up and move forward in the Newark Police Department. It was more than the image that was being portrayed by members of the Batons. The Batons were not bad guys. I don't want to make it seem like they were. But they had a different approach to being Black police officers in a majority white police force. When there was physical abuse of Black citizens by police officers, some of the Black police officers were too quick to be offensive to Black citizens. You also got the dirty work. You got sent to negative situations, and you had to be a part of it if you wanted to stay in the department. But the Bronze Shields began to stick up for Black citizens when they were brought into the different precincts. And they did not stand for police officers—black or white—taking physical advantage of Black residents.

James Du Bose: After we were an organization Floyd immediately filed several complaints and grievances to the Newark police director, Joseph Weldon. Director Weldon subsequently made some changes—punishments—involving superior officers he suspected of being racists.

Although the Bronze Shields was formed to fight for equal rights, not much would get accomplished without powerful allies to aid the cause. That changed when long-time New Jersey Congressman Hugh J. Addonizio decided to run for the mayor of Newark in 1962. Born and bred in the city, Addonizio won his congressional seat in 1948 with the backing of his district's Italian and growing African American population. Before his run for mayor the World War II veteran served as congressman for a total of seven consecutive terms.

Floyd Bostic Jr.: We had the opportunity to meet Congressman Hugh J. Addonizio, who had thrown his hat in the political arena. He was running for mayor in Newark. One morning during roll call, we were told Leo Carlin, the mayor at the time, was running for re-election. He'd sent word that traffic was not to assign any officers to escort Addonizio, who was campaigning. They did say that officers could volunteer. The assigning officer also warned us that anyone who volunteered to be Addonizio's escort would be doing so at his own peril. I felt at that time I had nothing to lose. So I volunteered. The job was for several days. And that time I got an opportunity to talk to him. I explained some of the unfair things I experienced. I expressed my concerns about the inequities of the Newark Police Department. I explained how discrimination against the Black officers created a breach in public safety. He listened, and then he made a promise. He said, "If you make me mayor, I will integrate the police department." I brought that information back to the Bronze Shields and, at that time, Charlie Harris was president. I told Charlie what Addonizio had told me that if we supported Addonizio as the Bronze Shields we would help ourselves. I believed Addonizio would keep his promise.

Thomas Murray: One day after a Sunday meeting of the Bronze Shields, we had a committee meeting with Addonizio about Black police officers wanting the opportunity to have different jobs and be considered for promotions. I don't remember what year it was but I do recall after that meeting Black police officers didn't encounter any more problems.

Harold Gibson: The Bronze Shields did have influence, but it wasn't as concentrated an influence as it would become later on. By the mid 1960s, the 4th Precinct was where most of the Black officers worked. But there were some in the 2nd Precinct on Orange Street.

Floyd Bostic Jr.: I recalled how I became a traffic officer in the Newark Police Department. I was working the dogwatch shift from 12 am to 8 am. And one morning about daybreak I began directing traffic at Broad and Market Street. I continued directing traffic for the three remaining days of my shift. Without my knowledge, a lieutenant had observed me as he drove across Broad and Market. He pulled over and summoned me to his car. He expressed concern over the fact that I was doing a good job although I was not assigned to traffic. He asked me did I want to be assigned to traffic and I said yes. In a few days I was re-assigned to traffic where, after a couple of weeks, I was assigned to the motorcycle squad.

Horace Braswell: Later, I got transferred and they sent me to a motorcycle squad. Even on the motorcycle squad I ran into the same thing. When I got there I could only ride certain motorcycles. They didn't want me on certain bikes because the white boys put their names on them. I couldn't touch it until every man had gotten his own bike. This happened for quite some time until we changed the regime in the department.

Junius Williams: I thought the Bronze Shields adequately represented the Black police officers within the city whereas the union, the Fraternal Order of Police (F.O.P.), wasn't really stepping up for Black people in the police force who were having trouble with the same police officers we were having trouble with. So I thought they did a good job representing the interest of that group.

If the Bronze Shields didn't have much to lose in quietly supporting Addonizio for mayor, they'd soon learn the benefits of backing the right political horse when he won. Shortly after getting elected, Addonizio's new police director Dominick A. Spina not only insisted that the Newark Police Department be integrated but he immediately promoted 10 African American officers to detective, most of the officers promoted were Bronze Shields members.

Floyd Bostic Jr.: Sure enough, Addonizio became the mayor. That November of 1962 Addonizio kept his promise. An order came from police director Dominick A. Spina that the police department was now integrated. Afterward, Spina promoted 10 African American officers to assignments that, before, were off-limits to Blacks.

Thomas Murray: They formed a committee of about three or four guys. And that committee met with the police director. That was a good meeting. It put the change in motion. It got guys where they wanted to be. The Newark Police Department began integrating. People began to get promoted to detective. I was one of the first Black police officers who became a detective, along with Floyd Bostic Jr., Bobie Cottle and Horace Braswell. That was after they formed a relationship with Addonizio. I'd say they helped inspire Addonizio to recruit more Black officers.

Janet Bostic: That promotion was Addonizio keeping the promise he made to my father to integrate the police department and promote Black officers. To get that promise, my father deliberately disobeyed his lieutenant and Mayor Leo Carlin's orders that no one volunteer to accompany Addonizio's campaign when asked. Do you have any idea how much courage it took for a 29-year-old Black rookie to disobey his racist, white superiors in 1962 on the chance of gaining access to a candidate who may or may not become mayor? It was a brave and brilliant move.

While this was a tremendous accomplishment, the historic breakthrough wouldn't appease a new crop of Bronze Shields members who'd joined the Newark Police Department in the early 1960s. Like their young counterparts battling in the civil rights movement, which would eventually turn into a fight for Black empowerment, these young officers didn't want symbolic gestures as much as they wanted Black officers to rise even higher in the department. After all, Newark had become a majority African American city by the mid-1960s. Along with eyeing growth within the Department, these new "young turks" also wanted to further change the relationship the police department had with the city's exploding Black population.

James Du Bose: Then the Bronze Shields got a new boost of ideas and enthusiasm with a set of fresh recruits like Hubert Williams, Charles "Pop" Knox, Claude Coleman, Clifford Minor, Carl Spruill, Daniel Blue and Frank Howard. Like many of the senior members, these new guys also became aware of the inherent racism in the Newark Police Department. It was apparent to them that the organization's way of dealing with the problem, while progressive, was a little stagnant as far as goals. They felt that the only way to affect the necessary changes was to take the civil service exams in order to become superior officers. To achieve this, they not only wanted to pass the exam, they also wanted to score high enough that it would be difficult to be passed over.

Charles Knox: The Bronze Shields was formed six years before I joined the force. And just about all the Black police officers were

Bronze Shields members. And there weren't a lot of Black officers —out of 1300 there were about 130 Black officers. And many of us were concerned about the discriminatory practices that existed as they related to assignments. At least some of us were. Then there were the young guys, like me back then, who were interested in elevating within the department. We wanted to be superior officers. But we were told it was difficult and almost impossible to do because other ethnic groups had access to the examination process. But a few of us who joined the Bronze Shields who were labeled "militant, young turks," didn't believe that.

Claude Coleman, Bronze Shields, NPD (1964-1991): We were known as the young turks. We ran for the presidency within the Bronze Shields. And we started bringing about a change in the organization. We would form alliances and support community organizations like the Leaguers, the NAACP, The Boys and Girls Club and other groups. And all that was fine. But we wanted to reach out and do more and we did. We worked with the Student Nonviolent Coordinating Committee (S.N.C.C.) and many of the progressive groups who were protesting and marching.

Charles Knox: When I went to the precinct I was assigned to, some of the Black guys told me about the Bronze Shields. The idea [of the group] piqued my interest. Then I went to a meeting and I was impressed with some of their goals and objectives. So I joined. The guy that impressed me the most was Hubert Williams. Back then he was just a police officer like the rest of us. But what really impressed me about him was that he was a man of integrity and he was concerned about people and justice in the community. He was also a very impressive speaker.

Harold Gibson: From the guys that I met, I could see this was an organization with forward-moving officers. They wanted to be more than just the guys in plainclothes or uniform. They wanted to go higher.

Claude Coleman: The difference was the older guys weren't confronting the system like we wanted to. They were happy where they were, I think. They were happy because they were taken care of, had made detective or they were doing a job they liked. The older officers liked being on the motorcycles or something along those lines. But our thing was we didn't just want to be the motorcycle guy or detective. We wanted to be sergeants. We wanted to be lieutenants. We wanted to be captains. We wanted to be police directors.

Charles Harris: There were other things we wanted to do in the department like get rank or obtain rank. From patrolman to sergeant, which was also a no-no for Black officers. Also, the white police officers always seemed ahead of us when it came to knowing things on the test beforehand. So Black officers were behind even before we sat down to take the advancement test. So we'd wind up 100th on the list. With that placement, there was no chance of making it. And even if a Black guy made the promotion list, where he was supposed to advance, they would stop the list or kill the list just to keep from promoting that Black policeman.

Charles Knox: We were the ones who thought the only way you can make changes in the police department was to run it and be in charge of it. Those guys were me, Hubert Williams, Claude Coleman, Frank Howard, Herb Friday, Percell Goodwyn, Clifford Minor, Carl Spruill and Harold Gibson. It was about 10 of us. We were advocating for study groups and efforts that would eventually put us in charge. That way, we could ensure that the community got better police service. That was our primary goal. But the older Bronze Shields members, the ones who were the founders, had limited aspirations. They were primarily concerned with becoming detectives, and they wanted to be on the motorcycles. To an extent, I could appreciate where they were coming from. During those times they did not believe that they could pass the exams and these were bright guys.

Claude Coleman: I didn't know about the Bronze Shields until I joined the police department. I heard by word of mouth about who they were and what they were doing. I heard it was a social gathering and they, as police officers, were trying to be part of the community where they'd come from. They were giving dinners and parties. And they were encouraging other Black people to join the police department. They were working on that too because they were trying to increase their numbers in the police department. And, in joining them, I found solace in being a part of the organization. Had it not been for them I don't think I would have stayed in the police department. Coming onto the force as a young person—as a young Black man—was a difficult decision. People like me were not inclined to join the police department. But I was talked into taking the test, solely at the behest of another Black police officer. He said, "And if you don't like it, you can always quit." So I joined. And when I found out about the Bronze Shields and joined them they made it a lot easier to stay.

Joseph Foushee, Bronze Shields, NPD (1968-1992): We met once a month, and we would talk about some of the problems we had in the department. Besides racial discrimination, there were also other issues we had, like identifying with the community. But not as a blue wall of silence. This was at that time when officers were committing serious acts of violence against minorities. We made up our mind we weren't going to stand for that and we weren't going to allow that to be done in our presence.

James Nance, Bronze Shields, NPD (1961-1989): The Bronze Shields were the only advocates asking for the recruitment of Blacks for the police department. They were instrumental in trying to help recruit Blacks through the church as well as media. But they went through the churches and high schools.

In 1963, the Bronze Shields became part of the powerful tapestry of civil rights organizations helping to organize the historic March on Washington for Jobs and Freedom. With African American unemployment at high levels and most Blacks relegated to menial jobs that offered no mobility, the protest fought legalized racism by pressuring President John F. Kennedy and his administration to initiate a strong civil rights bill in congress. Among the numerous police volunteers securing the march as well as the podium where Dr. Martin Luther King Jr. gave his famous "I Have a Dream" speech, Bronze Shields members saw their duties as police officers as a means to aid in the national struggle for equality. It further strengthened their commitment to improving their lives as police officers as well as the Black community of Newark.

James Du Bose: Before the march, a national plea was announced calling for Black police volunteers from police departments across the country to help in maintaining the crowd. When we learned about the march, the Bronze Shields requested that the Newark Police Department give us permission to go. The department refused. Many people felt there was no way you could get a bunch of Negroes together and not have trouble. They also reminded us we're police officers. Our response was, "That's the reason we're going, to help prevent any problems." They refused us a second time and we said we planned to go anyway. We were told we'd be in trouble if we disobeyed the order. But the day before the march, a teletype was sent to all commands permitting us to go. Unfortunately, all the buses were taken. We tried to find a bus to take us to Washington, D.C. Finally we were able to hire a small school bus with bald tires and a driver. Some members went by car and others went by chartered buses supplied by organizers of the march.

Harold Gibson: The Newark Police Department couldn't do anything about it. That was our private time, and that was one of the key issues. It had nothing to do with the police department. They didn't control it. They couldn't stop us from going. There may have been some who tried to convince their officers not to go. But no one was going to stop me from going. We had to rent buses. When we told the bus companies where we were going many of them didn't want to rent to the Bronze Shields because we had guns. Some bus companies just didn't want their buses going. Some gave us faulty buses. Some buses broke down on the New Jersey Turnpike and other highways all the way to D.C. Everybody knew this march was coming. Nobody knew how big it would be.

Leonard McGhee: We took a busload of Black police officers down there to do security around the podium where King and others were going to speak.

James Du Bose: I remember our bus stopped alongside the road, and some of the men had to relieve themselves. Forgetting that women were on the bus, the men suddenly looked up at the windows and saw the women laughing at them. But there was another time we had to go to the bathroom. We found a restaurant that was open in the morning. We got off the bus and went into the restaurant. Inside was about five or six rednecks at the counter looking hostile. We asked permission to use the restrooms, and the owner pointed to the outside saying, "The bathroom is out there." We went out back and there was nothing but a steep 25-foot ravine about 60 feet away. Needless to say we were angry. We were getting ready to go into the restaurant and tear it up. But a detective named George Alfred, who we respected, begged us not to get violent. He said that was just what the country predicted we would behave like. He also said we'd be doing do the march an injustice. So we got back on the bus and proceeded to D.C. A trip that should have taken us five hours took ten.

Leonard McGhee: We stopped in Delaware to use the bathroom. And the guy said we couldn't use it. And some of us were in uniform.

Thomas Murray: Despite whatever troubles we encountered on the way there, the trip down to D.C. was great. We had the white baker caps on. The caps you see people wearing in the footage. All the police officers had those caps on. The group I was in was lined up behind King. More or less you could call us security. And we all dressed alike in white shirts and black slacks.

Harold Gibson: I had a unique opportunity during the march. The "I Have a Dream" speech King made that day was changed three or four times before he said it. Just a few words here and there. When they would make a change to the speech, they would bring me a copy and I had to take it down beneath the stairwell of the Lincoln Memorial. So every time they made a new copy—and at that time they used carbon copies where the ink got all over your hands—I'd take it down. They had me do that like three or four times. Then I brought up the final version of the speech. They made sure that speech was just right.

James Du Bose: Once we got our armbands, we took up positions with other marshals in front of the National Guardsmen. Hundreds were standing at attention behind us along with an army of white policemen. The crowd was estimated to be 250,000 people. By the end of the march, there were 500,000.

Harold Gibson: When you see King making his speech, I was about 10 feet away from him.

James Du Bose: After being on duty for several hours, I got sick with stomach cramps because I hadn't made a bowel movement. I walked to a field hospital and they placed me on a cot. A doctor examined me and gave me something to stop the pain. Then they prepared to send me to the hospital. While they were making arrangements for me, I left the facility and went back on my post. I basically felt it was in God's hands. If I died while doing this, at least it was for a just cause. Fortunately, once I got back on the line, I started to feel a little better.

Thomas Murray: I was proud to be there and hear King speak and see all those Black folks. There were some white people mixed in. But it was just seeing that amount of Black folks. I was in the second row up behind Martin Luther King, Jr. I was located on the right [hand side] if you were facing the podium.

James Du Bose: When we were heading home, one of the things we discussed was the thrill of seeing Hollywood celebrities like Harry Belafonte, the actor James Garner, Diahann Carroll and Marlon Brando in person.

Thomas Murray: The adrenaline was very high. Everybody enjoyed it, although we were tired from working the march. Everybody enjoyed themselves. No complaints.

Janet Bostic: My father didn't talk about it with us. But what he did was he practiced. He had a reel-to-reel tape, and he practiced Martin Luther King's "I Have a Dream" speech. He kept saying it over and over and taping himself over and over until he memorized it. I mean he just loved it. My father later served as a bodyguard for Dr. Martin Luther King Jr. when he was flying out of Newark. My father took me to the airport, and I got a chance to meet him personally. I guess Dr. King told my father when he was leaving because it was very unceremonious when we met him. He didn't have a bodyguard with him. There was no Jesse Jackson. I mean he was there by himself. No fanfare or anything. He was just sitting up in a chair, back when transportation facilities had shoeshine stands. He was sitting high in this chair having his shoes shined when me and my father walked up on him. My father introduced me to him. He had this beautiful smile, and just said, "How are you?" He asked me my name and things of that nature. It wasn't a whole lot. He had a peripheral conversation with my father. I don't really remember but it was along the lines of, thank you for everything you did for me while I was here. And then he was gone.

James Du Bose: Ever since its inception, the Bronze Shields organization has consistently maintained, as a high priority, a commitment to the level of service to the Black community in efforts to improve the quality of life. The Bronze Shields and the Batons volunteered as ushers for the Mississippi Freedom rally, which was held at the Essex County courthouse at Market Street and Springfield Ave. The rally, which was on August 2, 1964, was called to protest the murder of three Mississippi civil rights workers James Chaney, Andrew Goodman and Michael Schwerner, who were killed in Meridian, Mississippi. For the rally we were dressed in plain clothes. But we could be identified by a red armband with the word "Freedom" on it. We basically kept order. We were told, for any unruly people or anyone causing trouble, to use peaceful, non-violent persuasion to either calm them down or remove them. The Bronze Shields president at the time, Thomas Hedgespeth, was the chief usher. Rallying against injustice in Mississippi was ironic since much remained to be done to correct the problems in Essex County and the city of Newark. There was still segregation in housing. Unemployment and discrimination in employment against Negroes was still commonplace. Schools were still, for the most part, segregated.

Chapter 2

STANDING ON THE VERGE
(1966-1969)

The year 1966 signaled a strong hint of change for the Bronze Shields, the city of Newark as well as the national civil rights struggle. That summer Stokely Carmichael, leader of S.N.C.C., injected the term "Black Power" into the civil rights lexicon via his famous Greenwood, MS speech, igniting a spirit of racial pride and determination among young Black activists while frightening many of their elders. Likewise, Newark had its political landscape tested when Kenneth A. Gibson, an African American civil engineer, entered the mayoral race against Leo Carlin and the incumbent Addonizio. The idea of Newark's first Black mayor was stoked when Gibson, who eventually came in third place, caused a run-off between his two opponents. In a city that officially had an African American majority, Gibson's run pushed against long-standing political loyalties with the possibilities of Black empowerment. This was especially the case for the Bronze Shields.

James Du Bose: When Kenneth Gibson first ran for mayor of

Newark against then-Mayor Addonizio in 1966, he quickly learned that he would need security. Harold Gibson, Kenneth's brother, who was a Bronze Shields member, provided security because political campaigns in Newark could get quite shady. The candidates would stop at nothing to win an election. The Bronze Shields had a policy against political endorsements. At first, we were reluctant to help. But Harold made an urgent appeal for officers to provide security for his brother. Along with Harold, other officers, like Carl Hargrove, Zeke Jennings, James Simpson, David Gordon El and Carl Spruill, volunteered. They reported directly to Kenneth's headquarters, which was located at Springfield Avenue and High Street.

Charles Knox: The older guys didn't support Gibson. The guys like Bostic and Millard and those people were well situated with their positions at that time. They were all detectives, which was a hell of an achievement. When they were just starting in the 1950s, that was the thing to be. You worked in the homicide squad or robbery squad or the Bureau of Investigations. Those were the positions those guys were interested in. They had good assignments and they fought to get there. But they didn't support Gibson. But we did, the turks did.

Harold Gibson: Of course, I was the one who wanted to support Ken in 1966. But Floyd Bostic and some others—without using the term white or Black—were trying to get us to support Addonizio. And Addonizio needed the African American police officers and citizens in the Central Ward to support him as opposed to the former mayor Leo Carlin, who was running again. In the mayor election, a candidate had to get 51 percent of the votes that were cast. Neither Addonizio nor Carlin got that 51 percent. Ken Gibson being in the '66 election caused a runoff between Addonizio and Carlin because they got the top two highest votes. When that happened, Ken Gibson was looked upon as a possible candidate for 1970.

Janet Bostic: My father's allegiance to Addonizio was because Addonizio kept his word to the Bronze Shields about advancing Black officers. Addonizio had proven himself. My father could not support Gibson publicly because he was being respectful of the man who kept his word. At the same time, my father did support Gibson as the first black man to run for Newark mayor. But he did so behind the scenes.

James Du Bose: During a Bronze Shields meeting we discussed political endorsements and selected the candidates for councilmen we would back like the incumbents Ralph Grant Jr., Donald Tucker, former South Ward Councilman Sharpe James and William D. Manns, Jr. We selected the candidates we felt had best served the community. Kenneth Gibson was the first of several unspoken endorsements of the Bronze Shields.

Thomas Murray: I didn't support Gibson at that time when he ran in '66. I supported Addonizio. I was afraid for my detail or my position at that time. You could lose your detail if you backed the wrong candidate. Back then there were a quite a few of us that supported Addonizio. And some supported Gibson secretly.

Charles Knox: Addonizio and his connection with the mob. They controlled the police department. They had their people in all the key slots. The head of the intelligence unit monitored everything. Anything that was anti-Addonizio they monitored. So Ken Gibson comes along. He's this young engineer, and he's challenging Addonizio. And, of course, if you had anything to do with his campaign you were a marked person as far as assignments and advancement were concerned. You were taking a risk, a huge risk. And them mobsters backing Addonizio, they didn't play around.

Harold Gibson: We did what we could within the police department. We even got some white police officers on our side because they didn't like some of the things in our department. And they didn't have much choice but to join the Black guys and let things happen as they were going to happen.

Charles Knox: Many of us didn't keep our support a secret. We did what we do. We provided security. Some guys made contributions. We worked for Gibson because we thought it was time for a change, and it was going to be our best effort to move forward. We owed it to the citizens of Newark.

Harold Gibson: We never had an organization meeting where we said, outright, we would support Addonizio or Gibson or Carlin. We didn't have that kind of conflict. What Addonizio did was name 10 African-American detectives. That was in his best interest politically.

Charles Knox: I paid a price for my support of Gibson in 1966. Oh yeah. But not just me. Hubert and Harold did also. But, of course, that was Ken's brother. We paid in subtle ways. For instance, when you are an officer and you work a rotating shift, instead of putting me in a car when you have two extra men, they would just put you out on foot by yourself especially when it's winter and freezing outside. Another example would be instead of assigning me to a radio car they might send me to the police academy to provide security. Or they'd just send me down to the cellblock to guard the inmates. That went on for a year or so.

James Du Bose: When the Bronze Shields was first formed, it was accused of being communist-inspired. At our third annual breakfast the guest speaker was civil rights lawyer Raymond Brown. During his speech he said, "I heard that the Bronze Shields was a communist organization. If the Bronze Shields is a communist organization and if the Bronze Shields are communists, then so is Ray Brown." Turning to Newark Mayor Hugh Addonizio, he then firmly stated, "Newark needs a Black Mayor."

Charles Knox: I was familiar with Ray Brown. I remember at a Bronze Shields breakfast he called for a Black mayor. We used to give breakfasts and dances to raise money for scholarships to give to Black students. But Ray Brown was a great man. I was impressed not only with his intelligence but also his Blackness. Ray Brown was a very fair-skinned Black man. And in those days color meant a lot in the Black community. There were very few light-skinned Black people who would speak out like that. So I was a little surprised that he got up there and talked about discrimination the way he did—and about the need for a Black mayor. I didn't know anything about him. I was surprised at how candid he was.

James Nance: Ray Brown supported the organization. If any issues came up regarding the Bronze Shields, and Ray Brown could speak on our behalf or talk about the Bronze Shields, he did so in the newspapers. He also spoke out for us in public meetings.

Leonard McGhee: Anything dealing with the law Ray Brown was there with us. He was one of three or four Black lawyers who helped take care of any problems the Bronze Shields had.

Junius Williams: Ray Brown was that kind of guy. I had been arrested in the civil rights movement working with S.N.C.C. in Montgomery, Alabama in 1965. They did not call my trial—I was out on bail—until the following year. I told Ray Brown and he was like, "What?" He got on a plane, came down and represented me at his own expense. That was the kind of guy he was.

No event precipitated change in Newark—its racial demographic, its politics, its police department, etc.—like the 1967 riots. The rebellion was one of many sparked in cities across America during that hot summer. And like most of them, what started it was an incident involving police brutality. A resident of a public housing project witnessed a Black cab driver named John Smith being arrested and beaten by police on July 12. Rumors then circulated that Smith died from his injuries, which weren't true. For Black Newarkers who were all too familiar with mistreatment at the hands of white police, this beating was *the last straw. After the crowds ignored calls for peaceful protest, the evening erupted into five days of burning, looting and rage that upended the city into a national spotlight. By the end of the uprising 26 people were dead, 700 were injured and $10 million dollars worth of damage left Newark immensely scarred. For many Bronze Shields members, the insurrection tugged at them both as African Americans who understood injustice and abuse dished by law enforcement and as officers hired to uphold the law. But in their quest to make changes in the Newark Police Department, the devastating 1967 rebellion turned into an undeniable launching pad for what they and the Black citizens of Newark were seeking.*

Harold Gibson: A couple of years before the riots, around the time I became Bronze Shields president, the idea of a civilian review board was brought up by numerous civil rights groups. All the officers were asked, "Do we or don't we want a civilian review board?" which would investigate any accusations of police brutality against Black residents. At the time, there was a separation between the white police officers and the Black police officers within the department. The Bronze Shields had a meeting at a place called the Bridge Club on Washington Street. We talked about how we were going to respond to the question. I made my case to the group for wanting a civilian review board. Most of the other police groups—the Italians, the Jewish, the Polish—said no. They didn't want the review board. Donald Harper and I led the fight to say yes. And at the end of our meeting that Sunday, we led the Bronze Shields in saying yes, too. But by the time we got out of the Bridge Club, someone from our organization had already gotten in touch with the police director and told him our answer. And the director didn't like it. As a result, the white power structure in the city was in total opposition to the Bronze Shields. Honestly, we knew they weren't going to agree to a civil review board. But we could afford to say we wanted it, especially if we stuck together. And that's what we did. The organization became tighter as a unit after that day.

After taking our stance, the department retaliated against us in subtle ways. But what would happen, say, if a Black police officer was accused of something or felt any supervisors in any way were wronging him, we would just go to one of the two Black newspapers, *The Herald News* or *The Afro-American*. Those papers started to write articles about what Black officers were thinking and doing.

Charles Knox: I had just finished a midnight shift. I'd just gotten into bed when I got a phone call. They told me to report back to duty. I said, "Wait a minute. I'm off. I just finished a midnight shift." They responded, "No. No. No. You report to duty. We got a riot going on." So I went back to the precinct. I was in the South Ward at the 5th Precinct. As I drove back to work, I could see people looting. Then when I got back to work, I found out what caused everything, the cab driver getting beat up at the 4th Precinct.

Harold Gibson: There was a lot of what I call false commentary before the riot. Then crowds of people began gathering around the 4th Precinct, and there was quite a bit of back-and-forth: everything from foul language to incidents between residents and the police. Across the street was a high-rise housing project where only Black people lived. So as the evening went on people began to break into stores, liquor stores, furniture stores and carry out things.

James Du Bose: Officers were told to hold off on making arrests until dispatchers checked with their superiors. A few minutes later, the dispatchers reported back that on the authority of Mayor Addonizio's office, not to make any arrests. Rumors circulated that the reason for the order was that arrests could hurt the mayor's chances for re-election in 1970.

Thomas Murray: The Bronze Shields did what they could do for folks in the streets. Protect them. Help them. Steer them from trouble and danger. When the riots started, I was at a birthday party for another police officer. I forget who came into the 411 Club where we were (at the time), but they said something like, do you know they're rioting on Springfield Avenue? They are tearing it up. That's when we all left the party to go see what was happening. I didn't report back to duty until the morning. By then they were calling everyone to report to their precincts immediately. I was a detective at the time, so I had to report to police headquarters.

James Du Bose: Shortly after the riot started it was ordered that, beginning immediately, all radio squad cars were to be integrated with Black and white teams—two Blacks and two white officers. That order to put Black and white officers together was the first in the history of the Newark Police Department. Before 1967 was the golden opportunity to start doing that sort of thing.

Thomas Murray: The Bronze Shields were very helpful during the riots. One day I worked 22 hours. Didn't go home. The riot in the streets was something. But they were fighting against racist police. There were racist officers and military officers. One white officer who was on the phone was asking someone, "Did you shoot any niggers today?" In fact, I rode up on cops beating up someone on Springfield Avenue. And I told them, "Oh no, you not going to do this."

Charles Knox: In the precinct, the cops were freaking out because we had not been trained. We had no preparation for a riot. So they were just handing out shotguns. And of course, the cops were really pissed off at what was happening. It was terrible because here it is, you have a lot of untrained people with shotguns. So there was a big concern about the safety of the people out there.

Harold Gibson: I was on duty when the rebellion started. Only, I was out of the West Ward. I was working at the 5th Precinct, which was in the South Ward. We were faced with the same thing, but not quite as bad because the rebellion was mostly concentrated in the Central Ward. We tried to keep people from doing things and making them understand that what they were doing was criminal.

There were times we sat with people on street corners and tried to get them to go home. Twenty-six people were killed during that riot. There was a woman, a grandmother, who was shot and killed in her kitchen on the 11th or 12th floor of the housing project across the street from the 4th Precinct. And out of the people killed during the riots, no one was ever arrested for the killing of anyone.

Junius Williams: The most egregious thing I witnessed was on Bergen Street. I can't think of the bar, but two young men went into the bar. After they went in, two state police also went inside the bar. These guys were looking for what was left after other people ransacked the place. So when they saw the cops come inside, they hid. One went behind the bar. The other just stood up, thinking he didn't have anything to worry about. So the state cops came in and said: "What do we have here?" Then they started shooting him. They shot him 46 times, including on the top of his head. We saw the body. Amiri Baraka had someone go and take pictures. It was put on a flyer, and the flyer was put up all over the city.

Thomas Murray: We stopped folks from looting. We stopped them. I didn't personally make any arrests.

Charles Knox: Most of the cops went out and arrested people, including me. I went out and arrested people because that's what we're supposed to do. We had on uniforms and that was our job, to arrest people breaking the law. I'm sure some officers didn't make any arrests. I know a couple of Black officers who came into the precinct and completely lost it. One, in particular, was later forced out of the department. He came in and was screaming that the cops were abusing Black people. He almost lost it that day.

James Du Bose: To the best of my knowledge, only one member of the Bronze Shields was seriously injured during the riot. That was Patrolman Shelly Gooden. He was accidently shot in the arm by one of his partners who was racking his shotgun in a squad car.

Charles Knox: There was a white police officer who'd gotten shot during the riots. He was Italian. His name was Frederick Toto. He got shot around the Stella Wright projects in the Central Ward. The question was who shot him. Of the prevailing opinion amongst the white police officers was some Black person—a sniper—shot him. But what we had in the city, at that time, was the National Guard. They were a bunch of civilians who were scared to death. They were firing indiscriminately at anything that moved. I was working a 7 pm to 3 am shift, and I had to go home from the 5th Precinct. I lived in the Central Ward. I was driving home in my uniform, and I had a National Guard man point a rifle at me. That's how afraid they were of anybody Black. As a result, myself along with every Black police officer who worked the 7 pm to 3 am made it our business to just stay in the precinct during that shift until daylight because we didn't want to get shot. Then they brought the state police in. Those officers went around to the Black-owned businesses that had signs in the window saying "Black-Owned" or "Soul Brother," and shot the windows up.

James Du Bose: Mrs. Eloise Spellman was killed on the third night of the riot on July 15, 1967. She lived in Hayes Homes on 18th Avenue. She died attempting to pull one of her younger children from in front of the window. She was shot in the carotid artery. The Bronze Shields immediately set up a trust fund of $18,000 for the children.

Leonard McGhee: During the riots, we had a family where the mother got killed and we pretty much adopted that family. We took care of them up to the time a couple of the kids went to college. We gave them money, groceries, whatever they needed. And if we found out there was a family in need, we went into our pockets to help them.

Thomas Murray: The riots destroyed Newark, especially my neighborhood near Springfield Avenue. South Orange Avenue. You know, a lot of the businesses were put out of business.

Lancelot Owens, Bronze Shields, NPD (1969-1981): I saw a guy on Clinton Avenue and Bergen Street take a wastepaper basket and throw it at a bank window. It bounced off, flew back, and hit the guy. I saw people going into liquor stores and clothing stores and looting. This was happening sporadically. It did not get to downtown. It just moved around the Central Ward. It tried to go to the North Ward where the Italians were, but it was mainly contained in the Central Ward.

Junius Williams: In the North Ward, Anthony Imperiale formed his organization. This was the start of this white vigilante group he led called the North Ward Citizens Committee. He also got headlines when he said during the riots: "When the black panther comes, the white hunter will be waiting." And he gained a lot of credibility within the city's North Ward. This was his coming-out opportunity. Eventually he ran for city council and won.

John Scott-Bey: Bronze Shields, NPD (1971-2005): I remember coming home one day and I wound up in the North Ward. And a bunch of Italian guys stopped me and asked what was I doing over there. I explained that I took the wrong bus when I was coming home from Kearney, NJ working a job. They said, "We'll take you home. Get in the car." I told them I wasn't getting in the car. It was Anthony Imperiale and a bunch of guys. One of them showed me a badge.

Harold Gibson: I think what changed after the riots were the businesses in Newark. I don't want to convey that, after the riots, all cops became good guys. That's not true.

James Du Bose: The riot ended that Sunday. Things appeared back to normal. New Jersey's governor ordered the State Police and the National Guard out of the City because a riot broke out in the city of Plainfield.

Lancelot Owens: I remember one day after the riot I was coming out of the Hall of Records behind the courthouse with another fellow named Charlie Hillman that worked with me. There was an Orthodox Jewish fellow in there with someone. He was filing an insurance claim or something. Outside the building was a protest march where people were carrying banners. One sign said "One Man. One Bed." Another banner said, "We Need Jobs." And one guy had a sign that said, "We Want More Money." When the Jewish guy saw that sign, he was livid. He shook his head and said in a Jewish German accent, "Dey vont more money. I can't believe it." When he said that, me and my friend laughed like crazy. I lost it. The Jewish guy saw they wanted more money after his property was destroyed and people took whatever they wanted for free. He thought that folks had the audacity to say they "vont more money." He took that sign personally.

Junius Williams: The long-term response to the riots was that white people left. They were already leaving, and the population was changing. The white population started going down in the '50s, when they used taxpayer money for highways and gave low-interest loans for people to move to the suburbs. That's really when whites started leaving Newark. The rebellions just accelerated it.

Thomas Murray: Whites had started to move out. They were moving as quickly as they could. But it didn't change overnight.

Harold Gibson: As time went on the Black section of the city just gravitated upward to eventually, where it is now, in the West and South Ward. But, before then, the East Ward was where mostly whites lived.

Lancelot Owens: What happened was people used to live in certain wards. And there was an exodus from the city that started before the rebellions. It started in the '50s. Black people were coming in and filling up all the neighborhoods. The North Ward, which was heavy Italian, became popular. As the Black population grew in the north, the Jewish community, which was most of the

South Ward, began moving to suburbs like West Orange and Short Hills. And when the temple moves, of course a lot of people move with the temple. That left a lot of vacant properties. So the South Ward filled up with Black people who came from the Central Ward. Then the West Ward, which used to be mostly Italian and Jewish, started going Black. With that, the city's political demographics changed. There was more of a Black voting mass. Whereas before Blacks mostly came from just one ward, now they dominated three wards. That became a growing influence.

Thomas Murray: When I left the force, Newark was a different city. Back then it was fun to go to work and to get off of work. Back in the '60s Newark was just a great city. You just had a good time because it was a fun city. After the riots, things changed. It was changing because they were trying to do different things with different organizations that were trying to get a toehold in Newark. They were trying to bring the city back to where it used to be.

Larry Brown, Bronze Shields, NPD (1972-1998): Back then there were very few occupations that offered positions for Blacks in Newark. There were public service jobs like the telephone company, the police, and fire department. Those were the major places that gave a sense of pride in the community because, before that, we were laborers and domestics. So organizing recruitment of Blacks in occupations like law enforcement helped in turning the whole community around.

Thomas Murray: There wasn't that much change in Newark. It wasn't like it was. When I was on the force, we had crime, but it wasn't like it was. By the '70s and after I left in '72, things got worse as the years went on. The people changed. But socially it wasn't bad, I still enjoyed myself. And the clubs were still jumping.

Harold Gibson: After the riots, The Bronze Shields started providing more community service activities for young people and adults. There were student organizations we began to work with and support. Stay-in-school programs were one. We'd also worked with groups to push children to go to college. Even police officers began to take advantage of college opportunities, which lead to getting young Black officers into classrooms and advancing in their careers. There was a place called the Leaguers on Clinton Avenue, which provided community programs and activities. We brought new doors for the building. We also started our annual dinner dance. We were going out to churches and schools, the YMCA and the Boys Club.

Charles Knox: That riot had a major detrimental impact on the city. It happened 52 years ago, and only 10 or 15 years ago did you see Newark starting to get back on its feet. The riot helped to transition Black people into positions that they never imagined. But, as far as the institutions were concerned, many people fled Newark. The reputation of Newark became infamous.

Louis Greenleaf: After the riots, they put out the report from the Kerner Commission. They started hiring a lot of Black police officers afterward. That's when I got hired in '68, right after the riots.

Charles Knox: After the riots, we young turks started going to school. Once President Lyndon Johnson petitioned congress to form the Kerner Commission to find out the cause of the riots across the country, and why the police weren't getting along with the Black community, they provided a lot of funds for education. As a result, a lot of us went to college and got degrees. Many of us got degrees in police science. We felt we were capable of running police departments. Those were our goals. And the older guys who formed the Bronze Shields, the ones who had limited aspirations said, "You guys are crazy. You guys are stirring the pot and challenging the administration. And we're the guys who are supposed to keep you under control."

John Scott-Bey: When I joined the police department there'd been a push for more Black police officers [to be recruited] after the riots. I wasn't here for the riots. I was in Vietnam. I came home in 1968 and worked. A member of the Bronze Shields, one of the originals, Bobie Cottle, was running around trying to recruit Black officers to join the Newark Police Department. He confronted me one day while I was walking. He asked what I was doing. I told him I'd just gotten out of the military, and he said I should join the police department. I said, "Are you kidding me? After what happened in Newark?" When I came back from Vietnam, I didn't recognize the city. Before the riots, Newark was vibrant. You could shop, buy food and go to bakeries. You could buy anything on Prince Street or Springfield Avenue. You had a bunch of movie theaters. But when I came home after the riots, there was nothing left. Everything was burned up. And I sure didn't want to be a police officer after I heard what happened to some of my friends who'd gotten shot up or locked up or were dead.

With the term "Black Power" firmly ensconced in the minds of Black Americans nationwide looking for control over their communities, activists in Newark were ready to change the shade of its city's power structure, especially amongst the leadership of its police department. It was a perfect opportunity for the young turks in the Bronze Shields.

Charles Knox: When I joined the Newark Police Department the city's population was close to 400,000. Right now it may be around 260,000. So, close to 200,000 people left the city over the decades following the riot. Politically the riots impacted Newark in a way that since then, every mayor of the city would be Black. The riots created opportunities for Black and Hispanic people. When I joined the police department in 1965 you could count the number of Black and Hispanic police officers on one hand. Blacks were about 10 percent of the department. Everybody else was white. But after '67, the majority of the police directors were Black. Though, that would take some time.

Joseph Foushee: White boys, for the most part, didn't work with Black boys. When I came into the department the average Black cop at a precinct couldn't go behind the desk. You were not allowed. I wasn't. The older guys were allowed behind the desk. But it was 1968, after the rebellion. So there was a lot of tension bubbling under the surface. The night Martin Luther King Jr. was killed, it came over the radio in the precinct about what happened, and the desk lieutenant said, "I'm glad they got that black nigger." Right out loud. But that was normal stuff you might hear in the precinct and no one would raise any eyebrows. I was a rookie. So when a white sergeant said, "They got that black son of a bitch," what was I to say? You had to stay cool to stay where you were. But, eventually, I was transferred out of the precinct because of my so-called militancy.

James Du Bose: Sally Carroll, who was the first president of the Newark chapter of the NAACP, asked Mayor Addonizio and Newark police director Spina to make Edward Williams the captain of the 4th Precinct. Since it was in the Central Ward, where the rebellion started, she thought the precinct could be better served if Williams was appointed to head it. She also said it would considerably improve the climate between the Black community and the police department. But it wasn't just Sally asking. She was backed by groups like the Bronze Shields, the Congress of Racial Equality, The United Afro-American Association, The New Jersey Baptist Convention and The Human Rights Commission.

Louis Greenleaf: Sally Carroll was one of the trailblazing women in law enforcement. She was instrumental in getting Edward Williams promoted. This was after the riots, when they put pressure on Mayor Addonizio to make Eddie Williams a captain and give him a precinct—which they did—to appease us.

Harold Gibson: Sally was one of the most influential police officers in the Newark Police Department—a tremendously influential person. And she was one of the first Black female police officers in the city. If you wanted anything done with Black police officers, you had to talk to Sally Carroll.

Louis Greenleaf: There was a police class of like 1,948 members when they hired about seven women because they didn't have any women in the department. There were about two or three Black women in that class. Sally was a part of it. She was also one of the leaders of the Batons. These female officers were dealing with female prisoners and stuff like that.

Charles Knox: Eddie Williams, who was a member of the Bronze Shields, became Newark's first Black captain. He was in the 4th Precinct. There was a lot of animosity surrounding that decision because at the time, the commanding officer of that precinct was a guy named Charles Zizza. He was a very popular guy, a good commanding officer. But it was on his watch that John Smith had got beaten almost to death, which started the riots. So the NAACP, whose Newark chapter was led by Sally, called for a transition from a white captain to a Black captain. But the problem was we didn't have any Black captains at that time. There were no Black captains. In fact, there were only three Black lieutenants. It just so happened that Eddie Williams passed the captains exam, and he was on the list. So Sally Carroll started this effort to get a Black captain and Eddie got promoted. As a result, they promoted Charles Zizza to inspector, which was a rank above captain. And they moved Eddie to the precinct. Eddie Williams is a brilliant guy. He had a photographic memory. You could ask him anything and he could give you the answer. That's how smart he was.

Floyd Bostic Jr.: Edward Williams became Newark's first African American precinct commander on April 11, 1968.

Charles Knox: The cops protested after Zizza was removed and Eddie Williams put in charge. The issue was, too, that Eddie Williams had a drinking problem. Nevertheless, there were a lot of hues and cries from the cops about that. But they're cops, and cops eventually get in line. So Eddie was commander, and he controlled all the privileges in the precinct.

Harold Gibson: For the most part, Eddie Williams was liked by most officers—white and Black. He didn't use offensive language or did things that were perceived as unacceptable among the officers. He talked to everybody the same, whether you were a superior or a rookie. He didn't let his rank get the best of him.

Heading out of the 1960s the Bronze Shields experienced a heightened profile that helped build their ranks as well as strengthen their influence within Newark.

Charles Knox: I can remember when the P.B.A. went on a sick-strike because they were concerned about money issues—pay raises and that sort of thing. The Bronze Shields said, "We're not going to do that." This was in the late '60s, after the riots. We were not going to call in sick, and we didn't. What we did was, on the streets, we filled many of the patrol cars with Bronze Shields members. My partner and I worked two districts because all the other officers called out sick. We believed in service to the community. At that time, there were a lot of Black people who required more services than anybody else. So my partner and I worked two adjoining districts all night long. And the Bronze Shields was doing that throughout the whole city.

Percell Goodwyn, Bronze Shields, NPD (1969-1994): I was a student at Rutgers University in Newark. I was attending a theatre workshop there and ran into a bunch of guys who were cops—Black cops. They were there for a meeting. I talked to some of them and afterward said that looks like something I need to be into. Something where I can try and affect some change. After fighting on the outside, all you're doing is running around with your dashiki on shouting "Black Power" and all that stuff. You just realize that all you're doing is spinning your wheels. That was my motive for going into the force and joining the Bronze Shields.

After meeting the Bronze Shields I decided to take the police exam.

Larry Brown: I was unemployed at the time, and taking a lot of civil service exams—postal exams, air traffic controller exams, air traffic marshal, the Newark Police Department, etc. During that time my appendix burst, and I was hospitalized. While I was in the hospital, I read a copy of *Reader's Digest*. What got my attention inside the magazine was there was an article on the Newark Police Department's Black police officers. I read the article and it was about the Bronze Shields. It talked about how the Black police officers organized because of a lot of racial tension in the city, and they were in the process of recruiting more young Blacks to join the police department. So, of course, I was attracted to that. The article mentioned Charlie Knox, who was the president of the Bronze Shields at that time. Once I got out of the hospital and was home I looked them up.

Thomas Murray: Hanging with the Bronze Shields was like going to a carnival. I loved the Bronze Shields. I loved the meetings. After I became an officer and joined the Bronze Shields I became the organization's secretary. The next two years I was the vice president. During that time Harold Gibson was the president.

Harold Gibson: We began to grow in strength because of our togetherness. The white power structure began to recognize that we were not to be messed with. They found our organization to be helpful. And, as a result, we were allowed to sit at the table because they needed our opinion. Even the guys who became the head of the P.B.A., which was a group representing all police officers, allowed the Bronze Shields to sit at their table.

Chapter 3

GUARDIANS OF CHANGE (1970-1972)

Once again Kenneth Gibson ran for Newark's mayor in 1970. Only, this time, he ran with the solid backing of a citywide constituency of Black and Latino voters, organized primarily by famed activist and writer Amiri Baraka. Unlike his 1966 run, Gibson had a supreme chance against the incumbent Addonizio, whose police director Spina had been indicted for failure to police illegal gambling two years prior. Among Gibson's supporters were some of Spina's top African American officers who, as members of the Bronze Shields, knew the importance of this mayoral race. As the city of Newark was about to experience a seismic shift in its racial and ethnic power structure, the Bronze Shields was poised to benefit from this historic change.

Louis Greenleaf: The Italians ran the city. They took control from the Irish. Addonizio was a congressman who'd become mayor with a coalition of Black folks who supported him against the Irish candidate. But in '66 when Gibson first ran, it was the start of us Black folks saying it's our time to run the city. It wasn't that Black people hated Addonizio. But under Addonizio, there was also corruption. We needed our own political leadership.

Percell Goodwyn: Once again within the Bronze Shields support for Gibson depended on the person's age. Guys who had been in the organization for a long time, like Norman Harris, believed they owed an allegiance to the powers that be—Addonizio. The old-timers were reluctant to get involved. Guys like me, Harold—Kenneth Gibson's brother—and some other folks, we were close to the future mayor. We opted to help him. We offered our assistance because of how it is in politics for a Black man. Gibson needed somebody to be with him. Basically, he needed a bodyguard. So I was a chauffeur and bodyguard.

Lancelot Owens: My joining the group came around the time when Ken Gibson ran for mayor. I also got to be the mayor's bodyguard during the campaign. We were working out of the South District when I got the call for that job. So I traveled to different neighborhoods and went in and out of town for political meetings and fundraisers.

Claude Coleman: I got involved when Amiri Baraka started recruiting folks to help Gibson run for mayor. After Gibson ran in 1966, which was kind of a disaster, that became an exercise for the next run. We got a lot of information for the next election. Instead of having all these people running for mayor, Amiri Baraka and his allies said we're going to decide on one person to support. We're going to have a community convention and decide who's running. We're going to have one guy run, and it will all be on that guy. Afterward, Baraka raised money for Gibson. The guys who were running for city council—he raised money for them too. He had people from out of town coming in to raise money like Jesse Jackson and James Brown.

Percell Goodwyn: After Gibson lost in '66, he didn't wait for the powers that be to give him their blessings. We, the citizens of Newark, formed the Black and Puerto Rican Convention at Clinton Place Junior High School. That was with Amiri Baraka and the Committee for Unified Newark (C-FUN). I wasn't a member, but I was there. I had just joined the police department, so it wasn't very good for me to be known as being a part of C-FUN back then. But I was also providing security at Clinton Place Junior High. This was after the Newark insurrection of 1967. That's what set me on my activist path.

Joseph Foushee: A lot of Bronze Shields still weren't backing Ken Gibson for mayor. In 1970, there was a meeting at a bar on Avon Avenue. In the back of the bar was a large dance hall. The meeting was to say whom the Black police officers were going to support—Gibson or Addonizio. Once again, all the young guys were for Gibson and all the older guys were for Addonizio—like Floyd Bostic, who helped found the Bronze Shields. In '59, before my time, Bostic was known as a rebel. That's why they started the organization. But by the time I came along, the Bronze Shields were not quite the rebels any longer. They were part of the older guys. They were not for Gibson as some of the other people because their assignments were pretty good at that time. And Addonizio was just placating them to keep his seat. So the guys who had those good jobs worked diligently to keep the status quo. And the way I read the conflict was young-versus-old. That was my perception. I came in as a young kid, and all these old guys were arguing about things I didn't understand.

Thomas Murray: The younger guys in the Bronze Shields supported Gibson. A lot of them did. There was Charlie Knox and Carl Spruill and a lot of the guys. The older guys like me, Floyd Bostic and Bobie Cottle, were close to Addonizio.

Percell Goodwyn: Some of the older guys, kind of frowned upon us helping Gibson. There was a little resentment but no hostility among the members. They just decided not to participate at that time. But of course after Gibson was elected, they wanted to participate and everything.

Lancelot Owens: Addonizio was a very likable man. As the mayor, he was politically street-minded. There's street politics, and there's politics on the job. He also had his favorites. I wouldn't call them political cronies, but he had his political organizations that he supported. And, to his credit, Addonizio supported some good Black organizations. But he also needed the support of the Black community. So he did a few things that supported the organization, which got him some backing. But people are going to vote the way they want to vote when election time comes. Also the population of the city had changed to such a large degree; it was a little harder for Addonizio to maintain his position as the mayor.

Charles Knox: I was Bronze Shields president from 1970 to 1971. And, again, when we supported Gibson we were under the microscope. The Intelligence Unit was looking at us. They had spies all over the place. You would see them standing around looking to see who was participating in the security details. They watched everything involving the campaign. They were preparing for retribution if Addonizio won. But we were out there making sure nothing happened to Gibson.

Louis Greenleaf: We supported Gibson without saying it. I was for Sharpe James who was running for councilman of the South Ward on the Gibson ticket. The police department didn't like us providing security for them because it was hell out there. It was war in the streets. Some guys faced off with white police officers. And if you were an officer working with one of the Gibson candidates, they would change your shift so you wouldn't be able to work with them. We were volunteering our time to make sure they had security, and nobody got hurt. That's one of the things that helped keep the peace; the Black police officers and the Bronze Shields provided security for the Black candidates.

Everybody knew us. So they could go and campaign without fear that someone would bother them.

Junius Williams: The Bronze Shields volunteered to protect Gibson because there was danger. I wasn't privy to any specific threat. But I knew it existed and that had been anticipated. You can't take a city like Newark away from one white ethnic group and just give the reigns of its government to Black people. This is America.

Lancelot Owens: Sure there was hostility toward Gibson. I had to look under his car for bombs. I had to keep an eye out for people that wanted to do things to him and attack. I had to be ready. There were constant threats. Gibson didn't ask for Bronze Shields, specifically, to guard him. He had a whole police roster to choose from. But during the campaign, it was suggested amongst the Bronze Shields that we step up and do what we could to safeguard the man.

Leonard McGhee: Working security for Gibson, we got rocks and bottles thrown at us. One time we went up to Vailsburg to a public housing building where all whites lived. It was for a rally. When Gibson got out of the car there were people on the roof throwing eggs and bottles.

Junius Williams: I remember having to ferry some people who were at a rally at a church in the North Ward. We had to go up there because Imperiale's people were threatening them. After the rebellion, poll workers for Addonizio—who were Black—had to run home because the white people were threatening them. This happened even though these Black people were on Addonizio's side. During that mayoral race, whites were very violent. It could be vicious.

James Du Bose: Carl Spruill, who was the Bronze Shields president, was transferred from his position as a detective. The reason for this was because Carl issued a statement during the Addonizio-Gibson campaign accusing Newark's police director, Dominick Spina, of lacking professionalism. In June of 1970, a departmental order was signed by the director reassigning Carl from the 4 p.m. shift to the midnight shift, behind the Lieutenant's desk in the detective bureau. Spruill of course obeyed. Spina said Spruill's reassignment was because of insubordination. Chief Anthony Barras said that a statement made by the Bronze Shields created a controversial situation within the department.

Percell Goodwyn: The problem was that the organization decided to go out and support Gibson during the election. We'd also go to the press and offer words. Dominick Spina took our president Carl Spruill, who was a detective, and busted him back down to patrolman. Spina put him back in uniform for providing services to Gibson and making a public announcement in support of Gibson. But we raised such a stink about it. By this time we'd learned the power of the press. We went to the press and talked about this. There was so much negative press on the Addonizio administration that Carl was reinstated as detective.

Claude Coleman: When we were escorting Gibson, I remember being with him one particular time on the campaign trail and he wanted to go to a police event. A police union was having a party in the Iron Bound section. He heard about it and wanted to stop by. We were like, "Okay, but here's what we have to do before we go." Because these police events were notorious for officers getting drunk and having ladies in the basement. The parties would get a little raunchy. We warned Gibson about that. So we said, "If we are going to go, we're going early." We stopped by and as I anticipated, it was a little raunchy. But we were able to get Gibson in and out without anything happening. I also remember driving with him through the community and people would throw eggs at us. We'd get out of the car to walk through a neighborhood and the eggs would come flying. This was in Vailsburg and many of the white areas. But Gibson was good; he was always appreciative, always in good spirits. He never got angry. I never saw him angry. Gibson was always upbeat, never down, and always smiling. He was very focused on what he was trying to do. He was very focused on what he was trying to do.

Lancelot Owens: We did have a silent block endorsement for Gibson. Of course the P.B.A. went for Addonizio. That's where it became a Black and white thing. But we liked what Gibson was saying.

In July of 1970, three years after the riots, Newark N.J. shocked the country again when it elected Kenneth A. Gibson as its first Black mayor. The win was the city's first move in changing the color of its power structure from City Hall to the Newark Police Department.

Junius Williams: As they were counting the ballots and it was apparent that Gibson was going to win—this was in the run-off—Jesse Jackson bussed some people in from Chicago. It was an election that was watched nationally. Students and labor people and movie stars from all over the country came here. Stevie Wonder came to help with the campaign. All kinds of people came here and contributed money. So on election night, Jesse Jackson had a bus down on Broad Street. People were standing on top of the bus. As the election was closing, the campaign workers came down to Symphony Hall to say Gibson won. We were going to celebrate. There must have been a thousand people in front of Symphony Hall just waiting for the announcement. And when the announcement came that Gibson won, everybody started singing the chorus to the Delfonics "Didn't I (Blow Your Mind This Time)." That was one of the most exciting moments in my life, and most certainly in the history of Newark.

Thomas Murray: A lot of white officers were not in favor of Gibson's win. That was until they understood there was nothing they could do about it. Gibson won.

Lancelot Owens: When Gibson was elected, I saw the reaction of a lot of whites in the police department. For them it was the first time they were in a position where they could be checked. And it wasn't like they could get away with different things like a 'good ole boy' system anymore.

James Du Bose: Ironically, Mayor-Elect Gibson said Director Spina's position would be the first one he would replace. When Gibson took office, Carl Spruill was appointed head of the Mayor's security staff.

Thomas Murray: I supported Addonizio both of the times he ran. When Gibson won, I was put back in uniform. Under Addonizio I became a detective. So if I supported Gibson and Addonizio won I would lose my detail. But Gibson won and I was back in uniform. I knew the game.

Junius Williams: When Gibson got in, he began to really desegregate the police department, which was still majority white at the time. He made sure more Black cops came on board. He did disappoint us by not hiring a Black police director at first. That was something people thought he would do, but he didn't. He lost points on that one. He hired John Redden, an Irish cop. I guess he had the support of the majority of the police who at the time were Italian. They would accept an Irish better than they could a Black man. That was Gibson's thinking. He wanted to calm the racial divide. Those of us who were less forgiving for what the police had done in the past, we wanted someone who was Black and who represented the people.

Percell Goodwyn: A lot of white officers responded to Gibson's win very negatively. But Gibson found a white police director, John Redden, who was fair enough. There was still that racism in the police department. But no one did anything like walk off the job after Gibson came into office. There were just grumblings. Once Gibson was elected, he started to make moves—bringing in people who supported him. I was one of those people. I got assigned to narcotics. Even though there was a lot of grumbling, Gibson also saw there were some white people on his side. He relied upon them for replacing those people who might have been with the former administration. There were also grumblings in the unions and organizations like the P.B.A., basically saying Gibson didn't know what he was doing. I didn't hear anyone say they weren't going to follow his orders. But I do remember one guy drew up some kind of paper trying to charge him with something. I don't know what it was. Maybe the guy made up something. You see a lot of crazy stuff going on, you don't know where it comes from. But you just hear it later on.

Louis Greenleaf: Now that Newark was a majority Black city, we had a Black mayor. But one of the white detectives said: "Let me tell you guys something. Yes, you guys won. But remember this one thing: a politician is a politician." And after he said that he left, didn't say anything else. We were like, "what the hell is he talking about?" We were treating Gibson as if he was absolutely going to do right by us. We treated him other than the way we treated a regular politician. We were fully supportive of the Gibson administration, all the way down the line. He was going to do this and that. We thought he would definitely hire a Black police director. But no, he hired an Irish guy, John Redden, as the police director. We didn't particularly care for that.

Joseph Foushee: At the time, I don't remember any uproar over not naming a Black director. Because at that time, people thought there was no one ready to be the director yet.

Charles Knox: Gibson said, "We can't move too quickly on this." In retrospect, he was right. But at that time, we as Black people were impatient. Although Redden had a reputation of being fair, he embraced many of the people who were our enemy, who treated Black people like dogs. Also, all of Redden's people were in all these top spots in the Newark Police Department. The police director before Redden, Dominick Spina, was controlled by the mob. So any change from Spina was an upgrade, especially for anyone with integrity. But we were still upset. So us militant, young turks challenged Ken Gibson in the newspapers. We challenged Gibson about Redden and some of the appointments Redden made for key positions. I was still the Bronze Shields president, so I was the guy who wrote the press releases and sent them to the newspapers. Afterward I was castigated. I hadn't been promoted yet, but everybody was after me for saying what I said. They punished me. They put me in all the worst places they thought an officer could be. For instance, they put me on a beat where the Black Panther Party had their headquarters and where the Black Muslims had a mosque. [They] put me on a beat by myself to walk. I think it was intended to try and get me hurt. But the thing was, I grew up in Newark—on the rough side of the mountain. And I knew all those guys in those organizations. But in the minds of the powers that be, the Panthers and the Muslims were supposedly dangerous people. They were public enemy number one to them. But that didn't mean anything to me.

Larry Brown: There was one story that said Ken's brother Harold was on the promotion list—the sergeants' list. And for years Ken held up promotions, and his brother didn't get promoted. We didn't know for sure if it was because he didn't want to promote his brother. But the fact remained that when his brother got on that list and was ready to get promoted, things slowed. The story goes that there was so much friction between Ken and Harold that their mother had to call them in to see her and she told Ken, "I don't care what you do but you better find a way to promote your brother." She made him promote Harold. I never heard anyone dispute that story. Folks just took it as true. No one ever denied it either. But the fact that Ken Gibson was the Black mayor and everybody respected that, no one tried to put him on the spot.

Charles Knox: That story about Ken not promoting Harold is not true. I don't know who said that but that's not true. I know. I worked for Hubert Williams who made the promotions. Harold didn't do well on the test, but Ken Gibson was never pushed to promote him. He was going to promote his brother. Come on.

Claude Coleman: Well, the department was changing because we wanted some things. At first, it didn't go that well. We wanted Gibson to make some immediate changes. We wanted a Black police director. He didn't do that. He appointed a white one. We wanted some people in the director's office. We didn't get that. I remember speaking up myself. The Bronze Shields also spoke to him. They complained he wasn't doing this, and he wasn't doing that. And I was like, "Hey, we got to treat Gibson like we would any other guy. And we can't let him off the hook because he's Black. We have to start using what influence and power we have to try and get what we want." That didn't go well with Harold, his brother. He thought we were prepared to put up a fight with the mayor. And we weren't going to fight the mayor. We all supported him. But we expected a little more from him than what we were getting. During that time Gibson was especially good to the Bronze Shields. We got assignments that we wanted. A lot of people became his bodyguard. I didn't want to be his bodyguard. He talked about it like that was a really good assignment. But a lot of us didn't want it—we wanted something else. We wanted to see a change in the police department. We wanted police directors. We wanted movement on the promotional scale.

Larry Brown: After Gibson got elected, the Bronze Shields were still trying to find out where they would fit. We now had a Black mayor. So a lot of people were trying to see how they could help and assist the mayor with what was going on in the city. There was still a lot of racial tension in Newark. The riots helped get the police department under control regarding brutality and mistreatment. And as time went on, more people were trying to address certain issues as they related to Black police officers.

Calvin Larkins, Bronze Shields, NPD (1971-1994): Under

Gibson the goals of the Bronze Shields didn't change. We were still about getting equality. Even though we had a Black mayor, most of the superiors in the Newark Police Department were all still white. It took a while for us to get enough Black superior officers. And if you weren't in the "ole boys club" you didn't get anything. If you didn't know anyone you didn't get anything.

Lancelot Owens: The whites had a buddy system. With the Italian and the Irish it was a matter of having an uncle or cousin on the force or in the fire department or in sanitation or the water department and boom they were on the job. That kind of favoritism was just interwoven in the fabric of the city and the political structure. So they were entrenched. But after Gibson got in, these other doors were going to get opened for people of color. And that old structure was going to crack loose. The wall of the old vision—which was mostly for whites—was going to change into inclusiveness.

In 1972, the Bronze Shields filed a discrimination lawsuit against the New Jersey Department of Civil Service. As one of many suits filed by Black police officers against police departments across the country, this was the Bronze Shields attempt to finally shatter racists barriers to advancement and recruitment within the Newark Police Department. The outcome of the case further changed the face of Newark's police force and its relationship to the city's predominantly African American and Hispanic population.

Claude Coleman: We found we still had to challenge the police department. So the Bronze Shields wound up suing the New Jersey Civil Service Department for discrimination, for its failure to attract other Black recruits for the Newark Police Department via the civil service exam. We also sued the city for not promoting the Black officers who were already in the department.

Percell Goodwyn: We'd learned how to advance our cause

through the courts by meeting with other police departments all over the country, and other people who had filed this type of lawsuit. We'd have regional meetings once a month. We would meet with officers in Philadelphia and New York. We'd have a delegation go, meet and talk. Then we'd discuss strategy.

Larry Brown: There were issues like making rank or getting certain police details or jobs like becoming detective or becoming a part of special units like traffic or narcotics. Narcotics wasn't a problem because they needed a lot of Blacks for that unit. But a lot of things regarding promotions became an issue. We began to organize and fight the problem by reaching out to other Black organizations in different states to see how they were making advancements and growing.

Claude Coleman: I had attended Rutgers undergraduate and was familiar with people at the law school. I knew Frank Askin in particular—Frank was a law professor there. He had a group at Rutgers that took on civil rights cases, and they were using Rutgers Law students for work on those cases. I talked to Frank and he took us on as a client. It was Percell Goodwyn, some others and myself. Frank's group would go and handle certain cases involving civil rights where the people filing the suits couldn't afford a lawyer. The students would help defend them. We gathered plaintiffs, and Frank interviewed them. Once we got Frank involved, we did very little. He handled everything. It was Frank's case and the students helped—they pursued it in court. He kept me abreast of what was going on.

Percell Goodwyn: I did all the investigations for the lawsuit. I found the people who had not been kicked off the police recruitment, promotions list, nor had they been hired by civil service. I had them go find their records and the results. I had to see the process in which they'd determined this person wasn't suited. I many cases, the rejection had nothing to do with their civil service test results. It had to do with the final personnel investigation. A lot of Black candidates complained they had been turned away. They were qualified, but for some reason the city had its own standards. And those standards were discriminatory in making a decision or not making a decision. And, for whatever reason—usually it was within a category called "moral turpitude." Maybe you had a child out of wedlock. Sometimes your credit was a little bad. Or, in my case, my eyesight was a little bad. Civil service found my eyes okay. I just needed glasses. So in the personnel investigation, they'd go over your background, your personal record, your military record, your birth certificate and all that stuff with a fine-tooth comb.

Claude Coleman: Black officers were getting disciplined for no reason while other officers were not. You had to go through the test and meet the physical requirements; you had to be a certain height. They required you to be five feet, eight inches in height. If you were Black and five foot and seven and a half inches you couldn't make it. But if you were Italian and [five foot and seven inches] you could make it. Or if you were some other group like Irish, you'd make it. But when you were Black, they became strict with the requirements. If you had a kid out of wedlock, that was grounds for being discharged. That was primarily used against us—not everybody else. So there were several discriminatory practices we discovered.

Lancelot Owens: They'd investigate you by talking to people in your neighborhood to see your social standing. It was also to see who knew you and what kind of person you were. But with the other guys, like the Italian guys? They'd say my uncle is so and so on the job and—boom— they'd be pushed right on through. But you had to run the gauntlet if you were Black. Your credit was also a big thing that came up.

Percell Goodwyn: Yes, some of the Black officers had good assignments. They had decent assignments like guys on the motorcycles. Some had risen to detective status but not a whole lot of high-ranking Blacks were in the police department. What would happen is this: Once those folks would get high up on the civil service list to get promoted or get recruited to the department, they'd see too many Blacks were on the list. And they'd let the list die or expire. The civil service exam is already competitive. That's to keep a lot of nepotism and favoritism out of it. They would let lists die rather than promote Blacks and Latinos.

Larry Brown: Another reason Black people weren't doing well with promotions was that the whites always seemed to excel on the promotional exams. Why? Because they either had the answers, or they had help from somebody somewhere with the tests. They also had study groups—which were run by guys who did really well on the test. So they started study groups. But not everybody could go to the study groups. To attend the top study groups, you had to be recommended. It would also cost you some money, anywhere from $1000 to $5000. They would guaranteed you would come out in the top ten.

Percell Goodwyn: I interviewed people I knew who'd been knocked off the list. I went out and talked to one plaintiff, in particular, who'd been knocked down the list for the Newark Police Department. Yet, he got hired by the Rutgers police. As a result, I saw there was some discrimination there. There were a variety of cases like this. Other people came in to join the lawsuit. They were people already on the police force. What I found was once they saw a group of Black guys on that list or more Black people than they liked on that list they let the list die or expire. I was a detective at the time. The other five or six people behind me in the case were civilians who'd taken the civil service test. They got rejected.

Larry Brown: In the end we won a mandate that stated, for every one white officer Newark had to hire two Black or minority police officers. That mandate on hiring minorities also applied to the promotional exam. These were things that the Bronze Shields spearheaded and won.

Percell Goodwyn: After I filed the lawsuit, I let the other people—future leaders of the Bronze Shields—handle it. I'd move on. When another person comes in to handle it, you didn't overstep whatever the president was doing. That's his or her responsibility now. You just move on.

Louis Greenleaf: Our lawsuit was like the ones filed in other cities across the country—Detroit, Chicago, New York. Those particular suits weren't won in the courts. But Mayor Coleman Young in Detroit settled his suit. The outcome was something like for every white officer promoted you have to promote a Black officer, something like that. Or for every white, you have to hire two Blacks—something like that. We were trying to get Gibson to do that and show him this could be our remedy.

Larry Brown: In the end they found the process was biased. It favored whites more than it did Blacks. That was one of the things that the Bronze Shields got together. It was a class-action suit that found that the practices were discriminatory.

Joseph Foushee: The suit also helped women who wanted to join the Newark Police Department. It changed our title from "policeman" to "police officer" because, following the suit, the doors were open for more women. And more of them started joining the police department. The change of the height and weight requirement helped lift the restrictive rules for women. When it was 5 foot 8 inches—a lot of women were left out. A woman who was 5 feet 2 inches could never be a police officer.

Leonard McGhee: After the ruling came down to recruit more minority officers, the people that did the recruiting were Black and Hispanic police officers. It was the Bronze Shields and several Hispanic officers who did the recruiting. Then, we trained them how to pass the written and the physical exam. We took them into

Branch Brook Park, particularly the females. We ran them and got them ready to pass the exam. We were proactive about getting folks on the force.

Joseph Foushee: Everybody who's an officer in the Newark Police Department—and is less than five feet eight inches tall—can thank the Bronze Shields for their job.

Kenneth A. Gibson, Mayor of Newark, N.J. (1970-1986): Once police officers got a chance to get the promotional examination, it was almost imperative to help get them into new positions. Even with the economic hardships of the city at that time, we still were able to make some promotions. And frankly, some of those officers were able to be successful. You had to be able to balance the economic problems with the need to do the right thing.

Lancelot Owens: When brothers started moving up through the police department, they were in positions to look at things that weren't fair and review them. That was especially the case when brothers started moving into the Inspections Office and Internal Affairs. There, white officers could eight-ball a Black guy and get rid of him or keep him from getting promoted.

Thomas Murray: They put quite a few Black officers in personnel investigations, which was to increase the number of Black police officers on the force. Before then, the Personnel Investigation Department was all white. But that changed when they put me in to do that job. When it came to those minor things that kept Black candidates out, I would say no. For me, it was a different ball game. I would approve them. They'd pass the exam. A lot of my guys who had those red flags for insignificant things came on the force and went on to great promotions.

Calvin Larkins: The police class I graduated in was the first time a class graduated with a majority of Black recruits. We had one more Black than white in the class. That was the first time.

Lancelot Owens: That was the next move, to buffer the system. That opened up the door and stimulated movement for Black officers to move up. It was more than an opportunity because Gibson was able to do four terms. As a result, the political strength of the Bronze Shields increased.

Charles Knox: John Redden was the director when the lawsuit happened. That situation might have been the thing that prompted him to eventually resign. He wasn't interested in any stuff like promoting Black officers. He was one of those guys who believed everything should be done on merit. With him, you couldn't take consideration anything like the totality of the problem, with education and the test being discriminatory. He didn't want to hear anything like that. He was one of those World War II veterans who walked around with his head in the sand. You could see this in the way he handled, or didn't handle, the controversy regarding the construction of Kawaida Towers.

Newark's police director John Redden as well as members of the Bronze Shields found themselves in the middle of another racial storm when white residents began protesting a Black-themed housing development called Kawaida Towers to be constructed in the North Ward. Amiri Baraka secured Housing and Urban Development approval for the building, which he named after activist Maulana Karenga's Black nationalist philosophy, Kawaida. The tower's African name, a Swahili word meaning "tradition," set off demonstrations which pit North Ward's Italian residents against Amiri Baraka and his Black allies.

Louis Greenleaf: Amiri Baraka came up with the idea for Kawaida Towers and got it through the council. He got everything done and approved. He got the construction started. Then when Imperiale and his supporter found out about what he'd done, they ousted the councilman from the North Ward because he signed off on the building's construction. When they marched on the construction site for Kawaida Towers, the Italians protested. And to keep order at the site the police were there. But we were telling Gibson to send all the Black police officers down there. We could keep things safe to get the building built. They didn't do that.

Claude Coleman: We'd run into Imperiale when Amiri Baraka was trying to put up the Kawaida Towers. We provided security for Amiri Baraka when they were starting work on the building. We guarded him when he was in danger. There was a protest against Kawaida Towers. There was a group who were in favor of Kawaida Towers and there was a group, led by Imperiale, who was opposed to it. They would march in protest and Baraka's group would march in favor of it. Of course we had police officers out there. But I knew Imperiale—you would just see him around. I was more afraid of his bodyguards and his colleagues than him. If you didn't go to the North Ward you wouldn't run into him. We didn't have a lot of groups in the North Ward. Nor did we have many, if any, meetings there. So the Bronze Shields didn't have any influence in the North Ward. Hardly any Black police officers were assigned to the North Ward. When we heard what he was doing there, of course we were opposed to it. But we never marched on him. He was just one of those guys that we knew of and disliked.

Charles Knox: I had just made sergeant when the protest over the Kawaida Towers happened. I worked in the North Ward. I was a sergeant working the day tour, and I had to keep many of those white cops in line. They weren't dealing with the protesters. I made the cops deal with them. Most of the protesters were Italian. And whenever I wasn't there the protesters got out of hand.

John Scott-Bey: I was a part of the tactical force. I worked on the Kawaida protests. Anthony Imperiale used to give out coffee and donuts every morning. He'd walk right past us and give it to all the white officers. We'd have to stand there in the crowd with the white people telling us to go back to Africa. Amiri Baraka would be there. And the white officers would always find a way to lock up somebody from Baraka's team, just about every person. Back then, there was a reporter named John Johnson on the Eyewitness News. He was there one time and got in the way. There was a scuffle in the street. He got in the middle of the scuffle. I was standing there with my nightstick. The white people were hurling these racist remarks at me like, "You're monkeys." And the other side, the Amiri Baraka side, would be calling Imperiale's people spaghetti-benders. My parents would tell me they saw me on TV. They were hearing all that mess. And we, the tactical force, would stand there between the whites and the Blacks so they wouldn't fight.

Junius Williams: To make a long story short, Ken Gibson didn't help Amiri Baraka finish the project. I think Gibson just left Baraka out there on purpose because he didn't want Baraka to be as powerful as he was. So as a result, there was a diminishing of Baraka's organization. His group was the last of the community organizations that had been a huge platform for Ken Gibson. They were the last of the organizations to begin disappearing because of a lack of support from Gibson once he got elected. That chapter was closed with the defeat of Kawaida Towers.

John Scott-Bey: To tell the truth, the North District was the worst place for a Black police officer to be. And if you weren't raised over there it was rough. Those guys treated you pretty bad. Even when I made sergeant the white guys thought they could talk over you and do what they wanted to do. And mind you, I trained a lot of those guys. But there was always somebody from the Bronze Shields you could talk to. My partner, Calvin Larkins, who I came on the force with, was vice president.

Louis Greenleaf: Everything came to a head, and the building never got built even though everybody had approved it. They dug the hole and laid the groundwork. But nothing went up. And the police director John Redden, rather than do something to help, would eventually quit the job.

Charles Knox: My press release, which criticized Gibson for hiring Redden, was the impetus for more scrutiny being put on Redden.

Chapter 4

BRONZE RISING
(1972-1981)

Shortly after the battle over the Kawaida Towers, Newark's police director Redden resigned, making way for further changes within the Newark Police Department. The most significant change was Mayor Gibson's hiring of Newark's first Black police director, Edward Kerr.

James Du Bose: After Gibson got elected, there was a mass exodus of white police officers to the Essex County Prosecutor's Office. A lot of them said they wouldn't work for a Black mayor or a Black police director. When Gibson gave notice that Edward Kerr, a Black officer, was being appointed as the new police director after Redden, the white police officers in the then 5th Precinct refused to go on duty. They said they weren't going to work for "no Black police director." Even the desk lieutenant, who was also the assignment lieutenant, refused to order the white officers on duty.

Harold Gibson: My brother Ken sent for the Bronze Shields. I was with him quite a bit. And I was in the police department. But what I tried to say to my brother was you need to get police officers to sit down with you, and you tell them what kind of city you want.

Charles Knox: The Bronze Shields was in great shape heading into the 1970s. You're talking about people who were presidents of the Bronze Shields who were set to move up in the Newark Police Department. Carl Spruill, who was Bronze Shields president before me, was the impetus for the moves that took place during the Gibson administration. To his credit, Carl was very politically astute. Unfortunately, he died young. He had a great relationship with Ken Gibson. He was in charge of Gibson's security in 1974. But he was diagnosed with a brain tumor that same year and died in 1975. He was very involved with the Gibson campaign as a strategist. He was also key to getting mayor Gibson's ear.

Niles Wilson, Bronze Shields, NPD (1990-2017): Maneuvering through that hierarchy is what the Bronze Shields offered new officers. As a new officer, there's only so much you can say about an issue, especially if you don't know anyone. But you could go to the Bronze Shields and they knew all these people. They could speak on your behalf if something wasn't right.

Calvin Larkins: During Gibson's second term was when the changes for Black officers started happening. He promoted a Black police director, Edward Kerr.

Louis Greenleaf: We thought we'd get an African American leader in the police department after Gibson got elected, but that didn't happen right away.

James Du Bose: There was one time I had to talk Kerr out of quitting the police force. One night in 1960 after his shift, Kerr was waiting for me at the precinct door, saying he couldn't take it anymore—the racism—and was quitting. I blocked the precinct door and told him I would not let him out without a fight. He said he didn't want to fight me. I told him if any Black officer could make it to the top of the department, it would be him. After taking the Civil Service test for promotion and finishing so high, he had the intelligence and preparation to do it. He couldn't be passed over, which was the unwritten policy of the department. Staying on, he could help change things. We shook hands, and he agreed to give it another try. The rest is history.

Anthony Kerr, Bronze Shields, son of Edward Kerr, NPD (1987-2009): My father becoming the first Black police director was a milestone, especially coming after Newark got its first Black mayor. When my father became police director, the Black officers were happy. But there were some issues. Back then the Newark City Council was five whites and four Blacks. You needed five votes to become the director. Every time they voted there were five votes against him. Then an Italian councilwoman named Marie Villani gave the swing vote in his favor. And my father got the position. Even then, the city was divided along racial lines as well as politically divided. During the time, my father became director there was a power shift toward the Black population.

Charles Knox: That hire came with controversy, but not as much as we'd anticipated. Kerr surprised me. When I first came on the department, he was one of the few Black sergeants we'd had.

James Du Bose: I remember when police director Kerr was assigned as my partner in a radio car, and he said he was interested in joining the Bronze Shields. In the interim, this was when he was promoted to sergeant and then to lieutenant. Just before he was appointed as Newark police director the subject of his joining the Bronze Shields came up again. He admitted to me that he regretted not joining the Bronze Shields before he'd become the police director. I also expressed my regret that he didn't join the Shields but, as police director, he was in a position to be of great support to the organization.

Anthony Kerr: My father was a tremendous supporter of the Bronze Shields. Before he was promoted to police director, my father was a lieutenant. During that period he never joined the organization, but he backed the Bronze Shields in whatever they did.

Percell Goodwyn: Ultimately though, Kerr didn't conduct himself in a way we thought he should as a Black police director.

Charles Knox: Instead of acting like he was commander-and-chief Kerr was very cautious in the things he did. He acted more like a lieutenant than a commander. Kerr hardly changed anything. The only things he changed were those things he felt safe to change. And there were issues to be resolved concerning the integrity of the Newark Police Department. For example, at that time, gambling was against the law. And there was a big bureau called the Bureau of Investigations. They were in charge of enforcing the gambling laws. But they weren't enforcing them impartially because many of them were on the take from the mob. So the people who received the brunt of enforcement were the Black people. The white gambling spots were not busted. And the people who were in charge of all of that were the people that should have been dealt with by us. But Edward Kerr did not deal with them. That wasn't because Gibson didn't allow him to do it. Gibson was the best guy you could work for because he didn't interfere in the police department. It was just that Kerr didn't do anything. That's why he didn't last in that position.

Percell Goodwyn: Edward Kerr would go on and do what any other white police director would do. And his appointment didn't suit us. It didn't suit the city.

Joseph Foushee: When Ken Gibson comes along in 1970 the times are still tumultuous. There was a mass transfer of all the people that were with him. And the people who were not with him came out of their good positions. That's normal. It happens in every mayoral election. But what occurred was that some of those people that weren't with him managed to stay. All they did was change their hats. Things did change. During that time, Bronze Shields's biggest contribution was how they pushed to make the police department truly integrated at every command.

Edward Kerr left his historic position in 1974. As his replacement, Gibson hired Hubert Williams, one of the Bronze Shields's young turks, who would become the longest reigning police director. Among his progressive policies was a strict rule of accountability for officers who fired their weapons. For a city scarred by its residents' anger over abusive police, this policy helped set a new precedent for policing Newark's Black and Latino residents.

Percell Goodwyn: Before Gibson's next term, he appointed Hubert Williams, who was a Bronze Shields member.

Larry Brown: Hubert and later Charlie Knox, were big on getting Blacks promoted in the police department. They were well aware of past discriminations we all experienced.

John L. Smith, Bronze Shields, NPD (1974-2000): Back in the 1970s, if you wanted to advance in the Newark Police Department as a Black police officer you had to be in the Bronze Shields. That was just how it worked. When I joined the police department in 1974, Hubert Williams became the police director. He and all the supervisors under him, who were Black, emphasized being a Bronze Shields member if you wanted to move outside of being a patrolman.

Percell Goodwyn: Before Kerr became Newark's police director, we'd recommended Hubert. But he was going to Harvard at the time on a scholarship. Hubert was gone for a year but when he came back from Harvard, he was appointed police director.

Calvin Larkins: When Hubert became police director in Newark that's when we saw a lot of change in the Bronze Shields and in the police department.

James Du Bose: In June 1974, when Hubert Williams was sworn in as director of the Newark Police Department, his first official act was to establish a new policy on the use of deadly force.

Bryan Morris, Bronze Shields, NPD (1981-2016): He had a policy that once I understood it, made absolute sense. It was his way of protecting the people of Newark. The policy was if an officer pulled his gun and fired it for any reason, the scrutiny on that officer would be relentless. You better be in the right for firing that weapon. You couldn't be "kind of right" or you "thought you were right." If you point your gun at any citizen in the city of Newark and shoot, you better have an absolutely good reason to do so. If you didn't [have a good reason], not only would you lose your position as a police officer, you would be criminally prosecuted. And the department wouldn't think twice about it. So because that type of policy existed in the police department, what did it do? It saved people's lives. It kept cops from shooting people like you see today. Hubert was a vanguard in reforming policy regarding a police officer's use of what we called "constructive force." Later on, I would have a conversation with Hubert about this and he explained the whole policy and why he did it. I mean, deadly force is a tool but so is just simply pulling your gun out on an armed suspect and giving him instructions. You don't always have to kill someone. As a result of that policy, Newark had the least police shootings per capita than any major city in the nation.

James Du Bose: As a result of the new policy on the use of deadly force, shootings by Newark police officers dropped dramatically. This led to the Newark Police Department being reported to have the lowest record on the use of deadly force in the country before director Hubert William's resignation in 1985.

John Scott-Bey: In the '70s we had Gibson behind us. So Bronze

Shields was doing things in the community. They had boxing. We did the P.A.L. I worked with that when I was working with the juvenile division, trying to do stuff around the city with the organization. But Gibson backed the Bronze Shields by pushing for more Black police officers. At the time we might have had four or five Black captains. He pushed for folks to take the promotion exams.

Claude Coleman: We had more power because we could do some of the things we wanted to do. We were pretty good as an organization. For example we'd give a big dance and we'd invite Gibson. He'd be sure to draw a bigger crowd than we drew before.

Percell Goodwyn: Maneuvering the police department was easier because my alliances were different. The people who knew me and the people who were important to opening doors also knew me. The person making the decisions—the administrators, the police director, etc.—knew me. So whatever I needed I could pretty much get it done. If there was a problem that needed to be addressed, I knew who to talk to. As the president of the Bronze Shields, you might see some guys get into trouble—as can happen to any good cop. I would be able to go in and talk—on behalf of the officer being investigated—to the police director. I could vouch for the officer's character. And that eased the way for a lot of people.

Harold Gibson: One thing I got to pat myself on the back about was that I never asked my brother for anything while he was there even though I was a lieutenant in the police department. I could have gotten easier assignments because my brother was the mayor. You can't be the brother of the mayor and somebody not come ask you for something. I remember one time I asked him to do something for somebody and my brother said to me very calmly, "You never ask me for anything, and I'm not going to say no to you but, at the same time, there can only be one mayor at a time."

Percell Goodwyn: I remember once when I talked to the press about the Bronze Shields. The next day I came in to work and the captain called me into his office and started to reprimand me. Then he realized I was the head of an organization, and that I can speak on it. That captain later came back and apologized. There's a policy as an officer: you cannot speak to the media without permission. But I didn't need permission.

Lancelot Owens: There was a rush by Black officers to get in the door for promotions. This was the first time, en masse, the Newark Police Department was affected by a racial change in its power structure. Some guys weren't used to having, say, a Black police captain or a Black deputy chief over them. So they might be like, the person in that position maybe white, but we have someone, racially, that's higher than him. And that went all the way up to the mayor. It sent a tremble through some of the boots on the department.

Percell Goodwyn: The Bronze Shields would organize a dance or we would sponsor carnivals or other affairs to raise money. And we'd donate it to the community. This is how we did things. I became a sergeant. While I was there, I was involved with the Bronze Shields for several years. I had a run-in with the police director. You know, politics. And I got busted back to being a patrolman. That's because I said something to Hubert, who was the police director at the time. And, before we got out of the meeting, I was transferred. But anyway, I was on the sergeants list, so it didn't make a difference.

Louis Greenleaf: When I got promoted in 1977 it was with one of the largest group of Black officers to get promoted at one time. I was promoted with Floyd Bostic. There were about nine of us. We had been trying to get promoted for years. We were on the list for four or five years—from '73 to '77. We thought it was wrong for the department not to promote us back in the early '70s. But when Hubert Williams became police director, we got more positions within the department.

Joseph Foushee: The Black Power people were very happy. The Bronze Shields did manage to move some guys into assignments they didn't normally get. The Bronze Shields flourished. One of the biggest things Gibson did for us was to allow for dues to be deducted from the paychecks. When that happened our treasury became flushed with money because dues were paid through people's salary. With that, it became possible for the Bronze Shields to buy a building or get a mortgage on one if they wanted. For a police organization to do this was unheard of. When the treasury was good the organization could articulate what it wanted to the mayor. We began to have his ear. We had a voice with the people who controlled Newark.

Charles Knox: The Black cops were happy initially. Hubert's promotion certainly had an impact on my career. After all, we were the militant, young turks and, all of a sudden, one of us was in charge. I was a sergeant and that changed my whole career because I went to work in his office. He had a major impact on the decision-making process. One thing I can say is that the Black police officers never had it so good until after Hubert became director. Any time someone Black got on the promotions list he promoted them. Also people were assigned to places they'd never imagined. He took care of people who did their jobs. And if you were a Black cop that didn't do anything, you didn't get anything. But all the guys who did their jobs all benefited from Hubert's tenure. There were more Blacks in the detective bureaus than ever before.

Larry Brown: Hubert Williams wasn't the first Black police director, but he was the first police director who came with serious education and understood police work. He became the president of the Police Foundation in Washington D.C. He was Ken Gibson's man. He ruled the police department, but he was very instrumental in changing the police department's image, getting into police-community relations, community policing and stuff like that. He was one of the up-and-coming visionaries of the police work because police work was changing. It wasn't about busting heads anymore or cops being involved in crime anymore. He cut a lot of that stuff out. He came and changed it all around. As much as some guys on the force might have hated him, he inspired a lot of them to further their education and rise higher in the department and beyond. A lot of guys who furthered their education did so because Hubert Williams pushed them to go and get their education. Some of those same people became influential in the department. People like Louis Greenleaf, who became an attorney, Charlie Knox and Claude Coleman, who became a judge. We were all in the Bronze Shields together. That helped change our image because a lot of the whites in the department weren't doing that.

John L. Smith: Hubert was sent to Yale to study. Afterward, he and many of his supervisors emphasized officers getting a college education. If you were trying to get a college education Hubert would give you work hours that wouldn't conflict with your school schedule. At the time, there were several officers, including the mayor's brother Harold, who were in law school and later graduated and admitted to the New Jersey bar. Hubert made it possible for those people to go to college and get undergraduate and graduate degrees. He promoted education as a way to better yourself as a police officer.

Joseph Foushee: Hubert was Gibson's most successful police director, and Charlie Knox was his right-hand man. So when Hubert left the position, he went on to take a national job. Charlie Knox became his successor. But Knox had a different management style. When he took over, he tried to rule with an autocratic, dictatorial, authoritarian rule. Do as I say and stuff like that. He challenged people in the police department—which made folks go to Ken Gibson and complain. We met with Gibson a couple of times to tell him Knox was not doing what he's supposed to. But when it came time to possibly pick a new police director, Gibson decided to stick with him.

Charles Knox: One of the big changes Hubert made was within a department called the Bureau of Investigations. It was a department that Kerr knew about but didn't really scrutinize. The officers there weren't doing their job, and they were on the take. What Hubert did was eliminate that bureau. Afterward, he entered into an agreement with the Essex County Prosecutors Office to have a small group of investigators investigate the gambling activities. And once he did that, Hubert's house was firebombed. The gambling guys were making money and Hubert cut their source of revenue. Also, a lot of money went down the drain for a lot of cops who were getting paid off.

Along with the community service programs and events, the Bronze Shields's basketball team helped raise the organization's profile as their games became a huge draw. The tournaments also built bridges between the Newark Police Department and Newark's grassroots community. In particular, the Bronze Shields's games against Newark's Nation of Islam's Mosque #25 team proved valuable at building a relationship between the two groups. Prior to this bond, there'd been longstanding tension between the mosque and Newark police. The bad blood was the result of a 1965 incident where, following a bank robbery and shoot-out involving two Black Muslims, officers raided Mosque #25 with guns drawn. The Bronze Shields's leadership wanted to help mend those wounds. Unfortunately that alliance was threatened when a rift developed between the mosque's leadership and a faction within the Nation of Islam bent on creating its own brand of Black empowerment. The end result was the death of Mosque #25's Minister James Shabazz, a trail of carnage, and a criminal organization that a member of the Bronze Shields helped bring to justice.

James Du Bose: When Kerr became police director, I met with him and asked for a favor. He had the authority to create a meaningful dialogue between the Newark Police Department and the Muslim community at Mosque #25. The department's reputation and image had been damaged because of a robbery that occurred in the winter of 1965 at the Robert Treat Bank over on the southwest corner of Seymour and Clinton Avenues. My squad sergeant, William Maiver and Mayor Hugh Addonizio's driver went to the scene and were immediately shot at. When Maiver was shot it left him paralyzed for life. The mayor and driver weren't hit. The suspects were identified as Black Muslims from Mosque #25, which was located at 25 South Orange Ave. A team of detectives went to the mosque and allegedly shot their way in. But once they were inside, all they found were women and children. I knew in order to repair the damage done by that incident, there needed to be a meeting between representatives of the police department and the minister of Mosque #25. That could possibly restore the community's confidence in the police department. Edward Kerr, who was police director at that time, Chief Barres and I met with the head of the mosque, Minister James Shabazz, at a Weequahic diner on Elizabeth Avenue. During the lunch meeting everybody agreed to exchange telephone numbers. The purpose was to notify the minister anytime police action was to be taken. The department could have free access to the mosque in search of suspects. Also, if the minister was aware of any suspects wanted by the police, the suspect would be requested to surrender to him or the police.

Charles Knox: James Du Bose was the ultimate diplomat. He was very smart, very savvy and he'd been around a long time. When he worked for Hubert Williams, who'd become the police director after Kerr, Du Bose was the contact between Mosque #25 and the Newark Police Department. He was the reason for the great relationship we had with Minister Shabazz.

James Du Bose: The meeting we had with the Black Muslims, when Kerr was police director, was a success. The main way we furthered diplomacy was a follow-up meeting where part of the conversation was about basketball. The Bronze Shields and Muslim representatives agreed since both organizations had basketball teams—the Muslim's team was the Bilalian All-Stars—we'd play a fundraising game for a 3-year-old girl named Jaida Davis. The little girl was in desperate need of a kidney transplant, which her parents couldn't afford. That first game was held at Barringer High School. We raised $1000.00, which aided Jaida's parents in continuing her dialysis treatment.

Larry Brown: You know Muslims playing police officers—that was special. This was back when most of the publicity about the Nation of Islam was that they were against the police. Muslims were always painted negatively like the Black Panthers and Amiri Baraka. We were out to prove that it wasn't like that. It helped build a lot of bridges in the Black community. The money would also go money to Mosque #25 to assist them in some of the things they were doing like helping guys coming out of prison. I can't begin to talk about all their programs for upward mobility and turning lives around.

Thomas Murray: I formed the Bronze Shields basketball team. And I bought the first set of uniforms.

Larry Brown: The Bronze Shields started doing a lot of community activities like going out and assisting the community with recreation events and helping out families. That's how we started going out and assisting people, by doing fundraisers. The big things we had were the basketball games. They were popular in the community because most of the guys who played on the basketball team were athletes in high school. So they knew other athletes. There were a lot of community basketball teams, and we started playing them. Those games became extremely popular. So the decision came to start doing fundraisers for issues in the community. We raised money to fight sickle cell anemia. That was a huge fundraiser. We'd fill up the gymnasium.

Percell Goodwyn: Claude Coleman created the Bronze Shields logo when he became the president. We had one and then we changed it. And Coleman changed it to the one we have now. We changed the decal in 1973 or '74. We also had the lapel pin. Everybody had the lapel pin, which brought some attention to you. We had blazers too.

Larry Brown: We played the prosecutor's office. That was a big game that gave us a lot of publicity. We played the Newark Fire Department. That too was a big game. We played the police department in D.C. They called themselves the D.C. Rollers. We even played the New York Giants. That was a huge game. And the more we played, the more popular the Bronze Shields basketball team became. We even joined the Continental League where we won a championship. That was a group of teams on the east coast, both police and civilian teams—and it became big. The basketball team and the Bronze Shields honor guard really helped a lot as far as putting the Bronze Shields on the map.

James Du Bose: In addition to being our biggest fundraising attraction, the basketball team gave the Bronze Shields high visibility and recognition. We played against other police basketball leagues in several states like Washington, D.C., Boston, and Connecticut. And we defeated them all. In New Jersey, we defeated the Camden Police Dept. We also held a benefit rock concert in the summer of 1976 called "Stand Up Rock Show." That was at School Stadium on Roseville and Bloomfield Avenues. Proceeds from the show were donated to a variety of charities, including the "Carl Spruill Memorial Center." Herbert Friday worked diligently to make sure the concert was a success. The performers on the program included Harold Melvin and the Blue Notes, featuring Teddy Pendergrass, the Moments and Crown Heights Affair. But the real blockbuster of the evening was The Ohio Players.

Larry Brown: Our annual dance, we can't forget about that. Every Black person in Newark wanted to go to the Bronze Shields dance. They called it the Black Policemen's Ball. It was always held the Saturday after Thanksgiving at the Terrace Ballroom. That started in the early '70s. We even gave a carnival. It was at School Stadium.

We gave talent shows. We had Kurtis Blow perform at one of them. This was before he became a star. We got a lot of supporters, especially the politicians. That's because of the large Black crowds we were drawing. So that brought in support from Black politicians. They always showed up, especially when we did things with celebrities like the New York Giants. All of that gave us a lot of credibility and influence as an organization in the community.

James Du Bose: We played four big games with the Bilalian All-Stars. The third game was played for the Sister Clara Muhammad School, which belonged to Mosque #25. The game raised $1000.00 for the school. We won that last of a four-game series. Proceeds were given to the graduating seniors from Science High School. Whitney Houston, who was 16-years-old at the time, sang "The Star-Spangled Banner" at the event.

Larry Brown: There were quite a few of us officers who were members of the Nation of Islam and considered ourselves Muslim. That helped bridge the gaps between the Bronze Shields and the Black Muslims. There was always a high level of respect for Muslims in Newark, which had always been that way. And we wanted to be a part of that. In Newark, Mosque #25 was probably the most active community that we had at that time other than the Black church, but none of them were as big and powerful as Mosque #25.

Claude Coleman: Some of us were asked back in the 1960s to be informants on Mosque #25. But we took a position we were not going to infiltrate the Muslim community. We were not going to do that. They wanted us to be a part of a team that kept an eye on them. But we said no, we're not participating in that. None of us in the Bronze Shields participated. We didn't go in and serve as informants and report anything on the Muslims.

Harold Gibson: We had to have a way for the Bronze Shields to build a connection with the Muslims. But during this time Mosque

#25 had its own internal conflict going on. It wasn't Muslims versus white people. It was Muslim versus Muslim. We were able to sit down with the mosque leadership and have conversations without conflict. Some of the Bronze Shields would even start training with the Fruit of Islam (F.O.I.) in martial arts. But when they had conflict within their own operation, that was another story.

James Du Bose: The relationship between the Bronze Shields and Mosque #25 was strong enough to be sustained despite the death of the religious leader, James Shabazz, and the appointment of a new leader, as well as changes in the mosque's religious philosophies.

Larry Brown: When the Nation of Islam leader Elijah Muhammad was in failing health there was a breakdown between a lot of the brothers who saw the N.O.I. more as an organization than a religion. That's what started causing a rift in the mosque. Out of that rift came a splinter group called The New World of Islam (N.W.O.I.). For them to move forward they needed leadership and money as well. That caused friction. And when they killed Minister James Shabazz, who was the head of Mosque #25, things came to a head. The N.W.O.I. were doing bank robberies. And one of their rules was in order to move up in rank with the organization, you have to bring back a cop's gun or badge. That caused a lot of friction between Black police, in particular, and the New Worlds. When we played basketball with Mosque #25, that was just before the split happened. Once that split happened things started to really fall apart.

Harold Gibson: Mayor Gibson was running in the park the day two headless bodies were found there. And the heads were found across town in an empty lot. That was quite an event. I wasn't involved with that case. But when they appeared there was huge conflict between the New World of Islam and Mosque #25, we knew it was going to be serious.

Larry Brown: I believe the rise of the New World of Islam had a lot to do with crime changing in the city. Blacks had taken over the drugs and number running, which helped push out a lot of the Italian influence. But the New Worlds was influential in a lot of the crimes that went on at that time. And remember the Italians in Newark came from the North Ward's Seventh Avenue projects. They were all Italians who lived in those areas. And they controlled that, even when you talk about the Vailsburg section with the Campisi crime family. The Mafia didn't even like dealing with them because they were considered gypsy Italians—who dealt with Blacks, Irish or anybody who wasn't Italian. But the New Worlds, those brothers came from Mosque #25, and they controlled the drugs. They were the ones doing all the bank robberies. Many of them were originally muscle for the Honorable Elijah Muhammad. Not saying that the Mosque was involved in the crime. A lot of times if someone from 25 got information that someone from there was wanted by police for a crime or a bank job, they would get the info to the mosque leadership, and they would bring that individual down to turn themselves in. If I had a problem finding somebody and I knew they were associated with 25, I would go there and put the word out that I needed to get to so and so for an arrest warrant. And because people knew me and that they'd get a fair shake with me, they would turn themselves in.

Joseph Foushee: The New Worlds seemed to be sticking up all the banks in Newark, the banks and supermarkets. Every Friday morning we knew there was going to be a stick-up. The only question was where. At the same time, all the stores along Chancellor Avenue were turning over from white ownership—Jewish—to Black ownership. It turned out that the guys doing this were also doing all the stick-ups. They were young Muslims. They would stick up the banks and the number runners too. That moment gave the Black Muslims in Newark the stigma that they were all bank robbers. I knew many of the boys who were doing this because we all went to school together.

Percell Goodwyn: The New Worlds trained their members to stick up banks. In one of their bank robberies in Newark, they killed a police officer. Because there were a lot of bank robberies, the FBI got involved as well. But we broke the case. When I saw the video of the bank robbery and other robberies, I saw it was organized. They had one minute to do it. Get in and get out. They were trained.

Joseph Foushee: They just went in like clockwork. Every Friday. And that push-pull between the New World of Islam and Mosque #25, I never got into the details of it or gained any intimate knowledge of the inner workings.

John Scott-Bey: I was involved in helping solve the bank robbery where a police officer was killed. I helped break that case. We had a task force and there was a kid involved in the crime. They showed us the picture and I knew the kid. He had that funny head. He was from the Weequahic section. He'd just been arrested. They wanted me to talk to him and scare him. I talked to him. When the New World of Islam robberies started, I was still working in Juvenile. They had me on the task force. We went to another detective who was in the Bronze Shields. His name was Ray Taylor. He worked part-time with youth. He said the kid was in his program. We went to the kid's house and his mother said she hadn't seen him in six months. We looked in his room. We searched the room. He had a bunch of IDs of people from prison in there. So we knew it was him. We got information where they were hiding out. The next day when I came to work, they had all the guys rounded up and sitting in the precinct—but we didn't know who the shooter was. They told me they got the kid from the picture in custody. So I asked to speak to him. As soon as I met the kid, he said, "I'll tell you anything. Just don't let them... They beat the mess out of me." I told him he'd be fine, but just tell me who was the one who shot the police officer. He pointed his head out the door and pointed to a dark-skinned kid. I asked, "But didn't an officer shoot the kid?" The kid explained that the one he pointed to was shot, but it was behind the knee and the bullet was lodged in his groin area. So I took the kid he pointed out into a room and him asked was he hurt. He said no. I said to him an officer was killed. He said he'd heard about it, but he had nothing to do with it. I asked him did an officer search him. He said, "Yes, they asked me to pull down my pants so they could look for the wound, but they found nothing." But I knew the bullet went behind his knee and was stuck in his groin. So I said, "Okay. I'm going to let you go," and then I patted him on the leg, and he screamed. I asked what was wrong. And he said to me, "Please don't let the white cops get me. They're gonna kill me if they find out what I did." So I asked him if he wanted to sign a Miranda. He wouldn't sign. So I wrote down everything he said and told Neil Patterson, who was in charge of the Homicide Squad. We actually got the guy confessing on tape. Neil pulled me out of the case and put in Bill Clark, who was also big in the Bronze Shields. We finished up the case and cleaned it all up.

Like most American cities, Newark completely lost its manufacturing base and, thus, much of its tax revenue. The city's goal of rebuilding its allure following the riots was thwarted by a budget crisis and all the negatives— failing education, growing poverty, crime, etc.—that came with it. In 1975, the same year the cover of the Daily News *blared the headline "Ford to New York: Drop Dead,"* Harper's *magazine tagged Newark "The Worst American City." To make matters worse, Gibson was faced with the inevitable job of cutting the police budget and laying off police, a decision that put the city at a disadvantage regarding crime. It began the slow unraveling of Gibson's good standing with the Newark Police Department.*

Junius Williams: During the first Gibson term, and maybe into the second, as the vision of rebellions across the country receded into the background, the money for cities like Newark began to decrease. There was no local source of money. Newark did not have the tax base to increase the level of spending that was necessary for better schools and better housing. The money just wasn't there locally. The state was not very supportive. They did what they had to do. And we had a Republican governor when Gibson first came in. And even though we had Richard Nixon in the White House, and he was surprisingly supportive of the city, the flow of federal money eventually stopped. By the time Jimmy Carter was elected in 1976, there was nothing left for cities like Newark. So Gibson had to wrestle with a whole lot of problems during this time. He was trying to keep the city taxes from going up. Eventually he had to use the federal money just to keep the taxes from going up on the local properties. Things had to be paid for. The mid-'70s into the '80s was a struggle. By that time the major businesses had flown the city and headed to the suburbs. In the mid-'70s there was still hope that we would turn this thing around. People were watching and hoping.

Larry Brown: Mayor Gibson was positive and negative for the police department. For some reason there were times when Ken Gibson appeared to be very unsupportive of the police. And to this day, I don't think many people even understood why. For example, there were a lot of economic issues in Newark as far as the city's budget. And Mayor Gibson always seemed to be fighting over the budget. There were a lot of cutbacks. One of the biggest things he did was to lay off police officers, which had never happened in the history of the city. It was gradual at first. It didn't happen all at once. The police department was a big source of revenue because of parking and traffic tickets. That's a big source of revenue for a municipality. And the department always had a surplus of funds for things like overtime because you don't know when an emergency would happen. But it seemed like each year when it came time for the police budget and we had a surplus, Gibson would take the surplus. And after another year he would take the surplus again—that would lower the budget. I mean, you might go a year or two without a major incident or emergency where the police are needed to do a lot of overtime. But what would happen is there wouldn't be enough money to do that. So you'd have to rob Peter to pay Paul. We'd come around to contract time and instead of us getting raises, he would give us an extra vacation day.

Joseph Foushee: During the years Gibson was in, he had to constantly cut the city budget, which meant he had to cut the police department. Not saying he didn't have to do what he had to do, but the budget was cut so much. That's why I became active politically.

Claude Coleman: It was rough, very rough. There was growing crime in the '70s.

John L. Smith, Bronze Shields, NPD (1974-2000): I was laid off twice. The first time was in '76, but it wasn't for long, maybe three or four months. Then again, I was laid off in 1979. That was a big hit, up to 100 officers were let go. It was all economics. I think the mayor was trying to force Trenton to send more money to Newark. But for most of us who were in school we were able to get employment with the city because of Hubert Williams and Ken Gibson.

Percell Goodwyn: I remember the city started to get worse in 1979 when there was a layoff of police officers. And there seemed to be an increase in crime. From my experience, I worked in narcotics and there were a lot of drugs flowing in—a lot of drugs. The '70s was one of the peaks in Newark's crime rate.

Claude Coleman: Gibson inherited the city, looking back on it. When he came in as mayor, the city was in pretty bad shape. And he didn't have a whole lot of power with the city council at that time. When you think about it, there was a limit to what he could do. And that was a little disappointing.

Lancelot Owens: I could see a dramatic change in the city. I remember what it was like when I was a kid—and I've run all over town. I would play hooky and have to run from the park police. Or you had to run from other gangs in town. Whoever was a member of this gang or that gang. This was in the '50s and the '60s. But back then throughout the city, you wouldn't be a victim going up and down the street. You wouldn't be preyed upon. But unfortunately, that was becoming the case in Newark going into the 1970s.

James Du Bose: Despite the fact that we had a policy against political endorsements, the organization backed Bronze Shields member Ronald Rice for West Ward councilman and Rev. Ralph Grant for councilman-at-large for the 1978 election. Endorsing Rice was special because he was the first Bronze Shields member to run for public office. And he won.

Lancelot Owens: I could see changes in juvenile crime. When I was coming up, if you got in trouble your parents had to come to the precinct to get you out. Back then, they had courthouses in each precinct. And if you were a juvenile, they would handle the case right there. Later on as the magnitude of charges involving kids grew, the system became overwhelmed. Then they developed a practice that if a parent could just come in and sign for the child, if the person signing was over 18, the child could be released to their custody. Then it got too much to just be handled in the precinct. I saw kids who were committing crimes like stealing cars, multiple times. You may catch a guy stealing cars or committing petty larceny. They were being released over and over. This was committing a bad seed amongst kids. Not that we were telling kids we didn't want to do anything to them for committing crimes. We wanted them to change their ways, but that wasn't the effect it was having back then. So indirectly, the system seemed to breed a subculture where if you got into trouble you won't realize the ramifications. So that made you a recidivist. As soon as they came out the precinct door the kid is like, "Thanks ma!" Then they'd run off and do it again. As a result, a generation of kids didn't understand the ramification of the judicial system until they turned 18. Then the jail bars are closing in on you and you need a bail bondsman to get out of this one. But by then it's too late.

Charles Knox: When Gibson became mayor a lot of police officers moved out of Newark. One of the things they did shortly after the riots was petition Trenton and the state legislators to reverse the rule that Newark officers had to live in Newark. Before that, you had to live in the city. But now all you had to do was pass the test and go through the background investigation. What Gibson was able to do was get a lot of federal funds into the city. For all the city workers who lived in the city, he put them on the city payroll. But when he hired cops, they were paid through federal funds. When the federal funds dried up then cops were laid off. That created an uproar amongst the police. It was a very difficult situation for Hubert. So what Hubert did was bring people in who were experts in reorganizing a police department. Hubert's tenure as director was tough. But he was a smart guy who had a good staff.

Percell Goodwyn: Despite the financial problems of the city and the police department, the Bronze Shields could really still get things done. I learned there's a way of doing things. I experienced it as the president of the Bronze Shields. We'd give a dance every year. And we'd have 2500 or 3000 people at Symphony Hall. And we always tried to get the politicians to come. Then, they would gladly come because they always got an audience. So we could get the politicians to attend and they'd buy tickets, so they could come in and mingle with the people. It was a ready-made audience. When you go talk to the politicians, they're more receptive to you for getting things done.

Chapter 5

Changing Shields (1982-1998)

The 1980s were a decade of growth and growing pains for the Bronze Shields, a period that took the group from being an organization to becoming a law enforcement institution. On April 29, 1984, the Bronze Shields celebrated its 25th anniversary with a special church service and candlelight vigil at the Metropolitan Baptist Church. A year before the event, the group officially planted its roots in the city, purchasing a building in downtown Newark which was christened as the Bronze Shields headquarters. The purchase was a logical next step in the organization creating a powerbase that could give it financial independence as well as a means of continuing its mission of uplifting Newark's community and lighting the career path of African American police officers.

Larry Brown: Trying to find the Bronze Shields was difficult if you were trying to join because they didn't have a building. During the time I was about to start the police academy and I was interested in joining. Once I was sworn in, I inquired about the Bronze Shields. I was told they met in the back room of a bar.

Leonard McGhee: We didn't have a home. We were all over Newark having meetings. After a while, the city gave us a building that went into default. So we decided it was time to get our own—for the Bronze Shields, and the community.

Bryan Morris, Bronze Shields, NPD (1981-2006): We met on the second floor of the building on Washington Street and William Street. It was a room up there. It had red crushed velvet with a red rug and mirrors. It was very, very 1970s. We used to meet there. After some time Leonard "Lenny" McGhee, who was the president at the time, and Calvin Larkins made the move to purchase another building.

Larry Brown: Before we got a building, we used to use the old Bridge Club on Washington Street. That was our regular meeting place. Purchasing a building was something we always wanted to do, especially after we realized the P.B.A. and the Fraternal Order Police (F.O.P.) had done it. Granted, those organizations represent all cops—mostly the white officers. We were basically mimicking them and following their lead on what to have for your organization.

James Du Bose: Along with being our headquarters, this building would also house many of our outreach programs. The Bronze Shields purchased its first building, which was located at 535 Martin Luther King, Jr. Blvd. Back then it was known as High Street. We purchased the building in 1977 for one dollar with the help of Pearl Beatty, who was chairman of the board of the Newark Housing Authority. That first building was in disrepair and desperately needed some renovations. Me and a few Bronze Shields members like Herbert Friday and Donald Deans did most of the renovation work. After we made the repairs, the members felt we needed to name the building after the late Carl Spruill who was a past Bronze Shields president. In addition to being used for meetings, the building would also have a community center named in his honor. We were in that building for two years. It had a small apartment that was occupied by Bronze Shields members who lived there rent-free in exchange for being the building's security.

Then the building's roof began to leak terribly. Soon the place desperately needed other repairs and we couldn't afford to have them done. So we stopped having meetings there.

Leonard McGhee: There was a piece of property we were renting from an organization on the corner of William Street and Washington Street. Then we saw this building up the street that was empty. So we contacted the owner. It was a lady whose husband just died. Since we were police officers, the lady told us we could have the building for $25,000.

Calvin Larkins: The woman who sold us the building had a business in it. Her husband, who'd died, used to work for the police department as a photographer. When she found out I was a cop, instead of renting the building to us she offered to sell it. She asked me if I was interested in buying. I said yes. The price was $25,000. You can't beat that price. The building was up the street from the place we'd been renting. And it was a better building.

Percell Goodwyn: For a while we tried to get another building. That idea went back and forth within the organization. One year you'd get an administration who'd say, "We want a building." Then the next group that comes in says, "We don't need this building." But we tried for a while. There was a couple of buildings we tried renting. And then finally in the late '70s or the early 1980s, the new president, Lenny McGhee and Calvin Larkins, who was vice president, brought the building on 43 William Street. I knew that place well. Somebody stole my truck down there one night.

Leonard McGhee: I took the idea of buying the building back to the Bronze Shields. They hemmed and hawed about it.

Joseph Foushee: When it came to buying the building there was a push-pull situation.

Calvin Larkins: Seemed like no one in the Bronze Shields wanted to buy it. There was a faction of the organization that did not want to do it. Why? I don't know. So we decided to buy it anyway.

Bryan Morris, Bronze Shields, NPD (1981-2006): I thought it was a great idea to buy the building. It was something we needed. But that's my thinking, "If you can own your own, why rent from someone else?" That's the way I was raised. I had parents and relatives who owned their own homes. Also, the money paid on a mortgage is the return on your investment in the future. If you pay rent, that money is simply gone. When we purchased the building it gave us a home. It was some place we can say—this is the Bronze Shields.

John Scott-Bey: I was the business manager when we purchased the building on William Street. They'd asked me about doing it. At the time, I was buying a lot of property—as much as I could. There were a lot of properties available because a lot of the white people, who owned property, were leaving Newark. I was buying everything I could. So Calvin and Leonard asked me about purchasing the property. I told them it was a good deal for the simple reason it was downtown Newark and eventually, it was going to be worth a lot of money.

Leonard McGhee: We went to our own personal bank and talked to the president of the bank. We knew him. We spoke and he said he'd lend us the money provided we put up some kind of equity. We didn't have any equity.

James Du Bose: After we all agreed to purchase the building Lenny and Calvin immediately went to City National Bank—which was Black-owned—to try and get a loan. But the bank manager told them, in order to secure the loan several Bronze Shields members would have to put up their homes as collateral. Because of that stipulation, Lenny and Calvin withdrew their already-existing savings accounts at City National.

Calvin Larkins: The Black bank said we needed crazy collateral to finance the building. I don't remember the whole conversation, but I knew it was ridiculous. They didn't trust us enough to give us a $25,000 mortgage on the building.

Leonard McGhee: The City National Bank wanted us to put up four houses for the loan instead of two houses. They basically rejected us. That's when we went to Hudson Bank.

Lancelot Owens: The Black bank we initially tried to get a loan from had acquired some trouble back then. The bank always needs someone to be responsible for the organization if they lend the money out, just in case the loan falls into default. Then someone had to sign for the loan. The strength of an organization are the principal parties involved, sort of like a corporation. Plus, we had had to get an organizational loan at that time. Point blank the Black bank wouldn't have been able to stand the shock if the loan went into default. So it was best to go to another bank that could handle it.

Leonard McGhee: Me and Calvin put up our houses as collateral. Our wives didn't know it. Hudson Bank gave us the $25,000 dollars and we bought the building. Shortly afterwards we went to the Newark police director and got a payroll deduction for all Black police officers in Newark whether they were members or not. They had to give up money to the Bronze Shields every month.

Calvin Larkins: When the guy at Hudson Bank told me what I needed for collateral, I thought that wasn't a problem because I know I ain't going to lose my house. Besides, we had income from membership dues and no bills. So Lenny and I made the deal without approval from the members. After the purchase, we had to do a lot of work on the property. The building was old, and the inside was run down. We didn't have to gut it, but we had to do the floors, the walls and everything. Eventually we got it together.

Leonard McGhee: The building was an old print shop. So it had photos and heavy equipment all over the place. We went to the city of Newark who managed to give us two dumpsters. Then, we installed a bar in the building. We bought all the equipment, and we also opened the bar upstairs in the new building. And we rented out the first floor to a guy running a catering business.

James Du Bose: The building we purchased was a social club called Club Mentors. Hames Mozelle, the owner of its A.B.C. license, sold Club Mentors to the Bronze Shields.

Claude Coleman: We got a liquor license. We knew a social group that had one. We're also a social group, so we bought their liquor license to operate as a social group.

Bryan Morris: There was some trouble in how we could name the building. As a police group there could be a liability if our name was on the building. You had to have another name for it. It was our building, but if our name was on it, we could be held responsible if anything happened in there. That's how we ended up with the name Club Mentors which, in reality, was already incorporated. Or maybe it was an LLC. I don't remember. I don't remember how it worked or how they handled it, but we had to consider the liability factor—especially with having a bar on the first floor.

Joseph Foushee: Many people thought we shouldn't buy this bar. There were several reasons. First, some believed alcohol is the root of all evil, and that we should buy something else. The main reason we wanted the bar was that it could maintain itself financially. It could provide a cash flow for doing the things we wanted to do. But other guys thought that owning a bar would be betraying our ethics as police officers. But owning the building never hurt the organization. In fact, it helped us immensely because it sustained us. It gave us financial independence to do things outside the box. We did Christmas mornings where we gave out toys. We cooked breakfast. We had fundraisers for various people.

Calvin Larkins: Once we purchased the building, I had a friend who had a private club license in Newark. And he wanted to get rid of it. So he sold me the private club license. That means members only. So we put a bar inside and had members come by. We had parties. All of that generated income for the Bronze Shields.

Percell Goodwyn: We may have had parties. For big events we would rent someplace else like Symphony Hall. But I only recall some parties. And that's because we had a bar there.

Lancelot Owens: Having that powerbase we could afford to take care of a lot of things. You could have classes for police officers. You could have afterschool tutoring programs for kids. We could organize all kinds of community efforts.

Calvin Larkins: Heading into the 1980s what also helped us financially was putting our members on payroll deduction, which the city didn't have to do. But luckily, they agreed. I had to go to finance and get our members' roster straight as far as what dues we were owed because we were being underpaid. At one point, the city was deducting dues but they were giving our dues to the P.B.A. So I had to straighten that out. A lot of guys are in the F.O.P., and that's payroll deductible, too. But according to our membership rolls, we were not getting all of our money. After we straightened that out, we were good from then on.

Leonard McGhee: The building was first and foremost a social club. It was opened every weekend: Thursday, Friday and Saturday. Sometimes we opened on Sunday. Members and their guests could come in, sit around and have drinks. We had food. All of it was for sale.

James Du Bose: The Bronze Shields held its first Christmas party at the new building in 1984. Detective Herb Friday dressed as Santa Claus and handed out toys and goodies to over 300 children. The event was sponsored by the proceeds from a previous basketball game that we won.

Leonard McGhee: When we purchased the building on William Street the Newark Police Department had a Black director. So the Bronze Shields didn't have the same confrontations we did since the old days when there were white directors. Back then they were trying to kill the organization. By the time we bought our building we'd had a Black director and a Black mayor.

Although the racial make-up of Newark's political landscape had changed since Ken Gibson's election, the Bronze Shields learned that remnants of political corruption remained. This was especially the case when, in 1982, Gibson was indicted for misconduct after a former Newark Councilman Michael Bontempo was awarded a no-show security job at a water systems plant where, from 1974 to 1981, he was paid a total of $115,000. The trial, while tainting Gibson's run for a fifth term as mayor, tested the Bronze Shields's (and Newark's) unwavering support of the mayor as many questioned the timing of the charges. Although Gibson was able to eke out another victory for re-election, faith in Newark's first Black mayor began to wane over the next four years. Gibson's reign would finally end following the 1986 mayoral race where he lost to the brash and outspoken South Ward Councilman Sharpe James. That mayor race, once again, caused a split within the Bronze Shields. But it also offered an opportunity for younger members to build their own professional bargaining platform within a new administration.

Harold Gibson: My brother and the city council president, Earl Harris, were on trial at the same time. They were charged with paying Michael Bontempo a no-show job. I sat in the courtroom during the trial. The jury decided that the lawyers hadn't proven, beyond a reasonable doubt, that neither Gibson nor Harris was guilty of any violation of the law. So they weren't convicted. The Bronze Shields made statements criticizing the fact that the indictments came so close to an election time for Gibson. That whole indictment drama was really on the part of certain political factions. They wanted to see Gibson and Harris on trial because there was a chance of them losing their positions.

James Du Bose: The Bronze Shields criticized the timing of the Essex County Grand Jury regarding the indictment of Gibson and Council President Earl Harris. We felt the findings should have been delayed until after the mayoral election. The organization put out a statement saying: "We are deeply disturbed at the timing of the recent indictments handed down against two top Black political officials in Newark. Mayor Gibson and Council President Harris were both candidates in the upcoming election.

Percell Goodwyn: I was part of that criticism. They always wanted to bring Gibson down. You had a situation where this old guy, Bontempo, who'd been in politics a long time, he'd been in the past administration with Addonizio. He worked for the city for years and years. They said Gibson gave him a no-show job. That's why Gibson was indicted. Gibson was doing this guy a favor.

Charles Knox: Those charges against Gibson were never founded. He was charged and there were allegations. But he was never incriminated. That never shook my faith in supporting Gibson, not at all. I thought the push behind those charges was politically motivated. You have to remember Gibson ran for New Jersey Governor twice. Once in 1981 and again in 1985. There'd never been a Black governor in the state. Now, when you're a Black man and you start talking about having that kind of influence, people are going to try and come up with all kinds of stuff. There were plenty of politicians around Essex County who didn't want Gibson to gain any additional power.

Percell Goodwyn: We thought it was unfair. They were just doing it to try and unseat him.

Claude Coleman: Yes, unfortunately, we supported Gibson during his trial. That was kind of stupid. All I know about that trial is what I read. I wasn't involved on the inside of that. I just heard when he was indicted for the crime. I thought what he'd done was kind of silly because we should expect more from our leaders. He was a Black leader, so to speak. And here he is getting elected and treating it like any other job like a white politician would treat it. So I was very disappointed. I don't recall us discussing the matter as a group because most of us were aware that Harold, Gibson's brother, was in the room. And no matter what he did, we still liked Gibson. The majority of us supported him despite what he [allegedly done]. And the guy he was giving the no-show jobs to wasn't exactly clean. I thought we'd gotten away from that corruption when we got Gibson in office.

Larry Brown: In the '80s the Bronze Shields began to change a little because it didn't have to fight the same battles as the '60s and early '70s. We had a Black mayor and a majority Black city council. We had a Black police director and Black police captains. So the organization began to relax a bit. It was becoming more and more like a social club. And most of the people in the organization were the old-timers. We were trying to be more political insiders than trying to deal with law enforcement issues and the needs of Blacks in the police department.

Junius Williams: I ran for mayor in '82 when Gibson and Harris got indicted. I ran because I didn't like what I saw coming from City Hall. I thought the people should be more involved and there should be an organizational effort to get the people back to where we were in the 1960s. I thought that would help get some support from the federal government and the state government. Gibson was still strong at that point, but that support started wavering during Gibson's next term. By 1986, the people were tired of Gibson.

Larry Brown: After 16 years in office Gibson fell out of grace with the Black community, especially with the police department. Everyone began slowly turning on him. That's how the tide began to turn. There was a group of Black officers who were primarily members of the Bronze Shields. They got together and sort of recruited Sharpe James to run against Gibson.

Claude Coleman: We liked Gibson. But like many, we thought 16 years was enough. He was running out of gas.

Louis Greenleaf: I was president of another police organization, and we supported Sharpe James. I thought it was time. We did five terms with Gibson and I didn't think we were going to get too much further with him.

Joseph Foushee: The Bronze Shields stuck with Gibson everywhere he went, including the 1982 corruption trial. But by the time 1985 rolled around, there'd been layoffs in the Newark Police Department. Gibson did this on two different occasions. The police were at the lowest level of manpower ever. The city was on its knees. And I started reading things about Gibson saying he'd had his time. Now it's time for him to go. I agreed with that.

Louis Greenleaf: We'd had just about enough of Mayor Gibson. Plus we had a falling out with him over numerous issues.

Larry Brown: We got together with Sharpe because he initially didn't want to run. He wanted to, but he was unsure that he could win. I don't think he felt he had the full support of the community. All of the Black officers, who didn't have great assignments, didn't outright back us. They supported us. But they wouldn't come out like me and some other guys.

Bryan Morris: Guys who'd been on the job for less than 10 years were thought to automatically be for Gibson. That was a different matter for older guys. Gibson laid off police in the late-70s. And the older guys were here for that. Under Gibson, a quarter of them got laid off. They took that hit and had to work their way back into the department. They were the affirmative action crew who did the lawsuit and got more minorities hired in the mid-70s. They were the ones who were let go and came back on the job in the early 1980s. They were the ones who were pissed off at Gibson. When Gibson was about to run for his fifth term a lot of these guys didn't forget the "fear city" campaign. That was when the police unions —I think the Bronze Shields were involved too—put out an ad campaign that told Newark residents that if cops get laid off the city is going to Hell. If you lose your police you lose the city. Fortunately, though, Hubert was able to do more with less. But he couldn't do that much more. Gibson was able to face a challenge from Earl Harris in 1982. But he couldn't survive the challenge from Sharpe James. By the time Sharpe ran, many of the cops who'd been laid off were now back on the job and not supporting Gibson.

Joseph Foushee: You had another schism brewing in the organization. Some in the Bronze Shields wanted to stick with Ken Gibson. Others wanted to go with Sharpe. But what happened was many of the people who had great assignments either stayed out of the debate or just stayed with the mayor. The political nature of the choice within the police department was who had what assignments. Those who had no assignments had nothing to lose. They went with Sharpe James. The rift over who-would-support-who almost came to fisticuffs in some of our meetings. The way we resolved it was like this: if you lived in Newark, support whomever you want to. But if you don't live here, stay out of the matter altogether and don't vote.

John L. Smith: The schism did not affect the Bronze Shields greatly. But there were some raucous debates. After that, there were side meetings among those who wanted to support the candidate of their choice. By this time, Gibson knew he was on his way out.

Larry Brown: Without our support, Sharpe wouldn't have won that election. One of the biggest things that assured him he had support was that most of the Bronze Shields guys like Al Spearman, Jack Holloway and myself were out front supporting him.

Percell Goodwyn: For that election, I sat on the sidelines. But Lenny McGhee and Calvin Larkins, those guys supported Gibson. Because I'd been around for awhile, they reached out to me later on. But I wasn't going to get involved in anything. During the mayor election in 1982, the police director busted me back to patrolman. He was one of Gibson's police directors. It was because of something I said. But with getting involved, you know the risk that you're taking. So for some people, it was best to just stay out of it, which is what I did.

Mae Smith, Bronze Shields, NPD (1981-2007): During the mayoral race the Bronze Shields had its annual dinner dance. Members who supported Sharpe brought Sharpe to the dance. This caused a minor conflict. There was a table for VIPs, which was for Mayor Gibson. But others argued that James was a "very important person," too. So they also let him sit at the table. There was no problem, but it was forceful. No one fought, but people were saying members of the Bronze Shields have a right to support the opponent.

Leonard McGhee: Me and many others were Gibson people. And the people who came out of the Bronze Shield who supported Sharpe—we had a few officers working in certain departments. They backed him. And when Sharpe got in, those who supported him became the leaders within the police department.

Larry Brown: When we met Sharpe James one thing he asked us was, "If you're going to support my run for mayor, what is it that you want?" That was our negotiation thing with him. We told him we wanted to be a big part of selecting who would be the police director and the fire director. Those were the people who have a large say in assignments. His response was, "Is that all you want?" We said yes. We also told him, whoever is chosen has to abide by whatever those decisions are, and we will support whoever is chosen. He said okay, and he kept his word. He asked for the names of candidates for police director. We told him we wanted Louis Greenleaf for police director and Claude Coleman as the fire director. Sharpe complied. When he named his cabinet—everyone we suggested was there. We had a lot of access and influence.

Claude Coleman: In '86 I took a leave from the police department and became the director of the fire department. Sharpe appointed me when he got elected. I didn't go back to the police department until 1988 when I became Newark's police director.

Charles Knox: Sharpe James was the guy that fired me. I was a Gibson supporter. When I became the police director, I eliminated some jobs in a few of the divisions. This put me at odds with certain groups of officers. I felt we didn't have enough people out on the street to deliver services to the community—not in a way I expected them to be delivered. As a result, I put 100 people out on the streets to patrol. Some of those people were Bronze Shields members. They were supervisors who weren't performing as well as I thought they should. One of them was Louis Greenleaf, who I'd known my entire life. After I eliminated those jobs, people like Frank Howard and several others, worked diligently for Sharpe James to get elected. The result was Greenleaf became the police director.

Joseph Foushee: For us, it was like a non-issue because everything went the Bronze Shields's way. Whatever we needed we got. There were no issues to speak of because Sharpe didn't drastically change anything from what Gibson had done. He picked Greenleaf, who was an active Bronze Shields member, as police director. He picked one of us, and there was no issue. Then came Claude Coleman, former Bronze Shields president. He was the next police director. Everyone was in step. My wife GiGi, who was also in the Bronze

Shields, and I were there for Sharpe's first term. But by the time he got to his second term, we were gone. To tell the truth, Sharpe is a whole other conversation.

James ran with the slogan "Newark Needs A Sharpe Change." Among the changes he'd promised was to seriously deal with one of Newark's biggest issues, crime. Violent crimes and drugs had become a huge problem under the Gibson administration, which had been bogged down with balancing the city's depleting budget. Under a new plan to fight crime, James promised to improve police services, which he did by mandating a stronger coalition between the Newark Police Department and residents. Numerous members of the Bronze Shields played key roles in this attempt. This was crucial because from the late '80s into the early 1990s, Newark was also becoming known as the "stolen car capital of the country." In 1992, 111 people were killed in the city in car-theft related incidents.

Claude Coleman: Sharpe gave directives. He had a lot of them at that time. When I came on, the city was deluged with stolen cars and other crimes. A lot of calls to the police department were going unanswered. Dealing with the lack of police services was one of the things Sharpe ran on. Crime was getting rampant. We needed to take care of all that stuff. So when he became mayor, my duties became the fire department. But when I became police director that's when he had more to talk about. He wanted an increase in services.

Louis Greenleaf: When I became police director under Sharpe, we assembled a Community Relations Bureau which put together the community-policing project. We started that program in the late '70s. I was in charge of the community relations/crime prevention unit. You had to go out and visit with different block watch groups and get the city involved. We had units all over the city. We recruited community members to do certain things. If something happened in the neighborhood, we would go in and straighten it out, without having to send in the troops. There were no issues between the community and the police during that time, which was great. But some issues needed to be solved. I thought we needed to emphasize community. I made my guys go to different communities and talk to the people and find out what their problems were so we could try and solve them. You can't police an area if you don't know the people.

Mae Smith, Bronze Shields, NPD (1981-2007): Under Sharpe James I became a detective. I worked in crime prevention, which was part of the Community Relations Department.

Bryan Morris: We had a crime prevention unit. That unit was always mostly Black because the city was mostly Black. There was a sprinkling of Italian or Latino guys working the unit. But, generally, it was a Black operation. No matter what color you were, if you worked in that unit you had to have some level of social consciousness to be effective. Everyone understood that automatically. It was about protecting the community and not having that us-versus-them approach. We had to really keep that in mind when drug dealing became a huge problem in Newark.

Percell Goodwyn: The crack issue was bad. I did a stint with the DEA back then. It was bad. And I couldn't understand it. I worked narcotics before there was such a thing called crack. When that drug hit, I couldn't understand why. But after a while I saw why—it was so addictive. People smoke it one time and were hooked.

Mae Smith: When the crack epidemic came that's when the crime seemed to spike.

Bryan Morris: When Charlie Knox became police director, he implemented drug testing in the Newark Police Department. Why? A lot of cops were out there using narcotics. Remember, this was the 1980s and snorting cocaine was the in thing. People weren't just smoking pot. These cats were getting high. Because of the drug policy, that had to stop. If you got caught, you didn't get put on probation. If you took a urine test and it came back hot you got fired. He just threw you out the door. You were done.

Levi A. Holmes II, Bronze Shields, NPD (1992-2019): When I joined the department Newark was the stolen car capital of the country. People were stealing cars all over the place and driving around crazily. Street crime was on the rise, including robberies, and things of that nature. I was even the victim of armed robbery three times.

Joseph Foushee: I don't know what caused the stolen car epidemic. But I can say this: if you're in the suburbs living a middleclass lifestyle, and you have a 13-year-old or a 14-year-old son, and he's sitting on the back porch all day long and has nothing to do. He will find something to do. You'd get him involved in the sports program. They're playing baseball or basketball games on Saturday morning. They have to get up early to play. So more than likely there isn't much negativity they can get into. At the same time, kids will get into dangerous things whether you supervise them or not. But in Newark like a lot of poor cities and towns, we have a bunch of boys who have no father figures. It was the idleness and a lack of life and spiritual guidance. I remember an incident that happened while we were working with Sharpe James when he was campaigning for mayor. One night we were on Hawthorne Avenue and Osborne Terrace. A kid in a stolen car came up Hawthorne Avenue. He was speeding. He tried to make a quick turn, but he couldn't. He jumped the curb and hit a kid sitting on a stoop on the opposite corner. He cut the kid totally in half and killed him. Me and two other officers were waiting for Sharpe to give his speech and we see this happen. I catch the kid driving the stolen car, and he does not have any idea about what he did. And when we told him what happened he had no comprehension of what he'd just done. I tried to talk to him, but it was like talking to an alien. He had no clue. So when people ask what caused the stolen car epidemic, I think about the kids sitting around do nothing. But at the same time, the city also failed the kids because the police department was at its lowest level of manpower. By the time Sharpe James took office, the police department had around 800 cops for the entire city of Newark. When I first joined the force in 1968 there were 1600.

Larry Brown: One way we fought the stolen car epidemic was we had an auto-theft prevention program. We received some federal funds for it. With the money, one of the things we were able to do was to purchase anti-theft devices, the Clubs. We gave hundreds of them away. That helped. But as those funds dried up and things changed in the schools—the cutting of truancy programs—the kids started being out in the streets. Of course, that leads to an increase in crime—especially auto theft. That increased drastically.

Anthony Kerr: When Newark became the stolen car capital I worked in juvenile at the time. I got to interact with a lot of the offenders. Me and a small group of detectives who were conscious and community-minded helped provide direction, guidance and counseling for a lot of those juveniles coming in for stolen cars. We'd talk to them before they were released to their guardians. There were hundreds of kids coming in. The youngest I saw was 8 years old. He was reported to be sitting on milk crates while driving a stolen car. Me and these detectives had our own philosophy. We felt we had to do something because the situation was really out of control. Youths would come in knowing they'd be released. So they had no problems telling you, "Shut the fuck up." We had to change that whole mentality and help them see that when they came here, this was our house. And you're going to respect our house as if it were your own. After talking to the kids we learned that 95 percent of them didn't have a father in the house. Either they didn't know the father, or he was in jail or dead. So we tried to take on that fatherly role and set some disciplinary parameters. We told those kids if they continued doing these destructive things, we were going to treat them like a father would treat you. I think we were successful because our recidivist rate began to go down. Also, the word on the street was if you get busted and sent down to youth house, don't think you're getting a pass anymore. 'Them brothers' are waiting for you. We were all on board with the same mission, to help turn these kids around. It was just out of control.

Bryan Morris: If you were conscious of the community you had to keep the humanity of everyone affected by that stolen epidemic in mind. In 1991, there was a young black girl, Tasha Maysey, who was shot and killed by Newark and Hillside police after riding in a stolen van. Newark police were chasing the van. There were five or six kids in the vehicle, including Maysey. The van went into Hillside, NJ via a bridge that was blocked off on the other side. The kids stopped the van and got out. The cops said they saw a gun and opened fire. Maysey, 17-years-old, was killed along with a 20-year-old guy named Lamont Russell Jones. Afterward, there was an uproar. I'm sitting in a meeting of police, planning how to deal with this. The department says they're putting cops here and there to keep things quiet. We're told if we see certain people, intelligence will keep an eye on them. In my ignorance, I asked the then police director, William Celester, "Has anyone gone up and talked to this girl's family while all this proactive planning is going on?" I said, "If the people are planning a march and we're planning to address the march, it would be reasonable to ask the family how we can help. We can offer our condolences. They looked at me like I had six heads. They said, "Mr. Morris, since this is your brilliant idea, why don't you go and do it." I said sure. So I put on my full uniform and went up to Tasha's family apartment in Hill Manor on High Street. I went up to the door and knocked. A guy answered the door. I introduce myself and told him I was there to first off, offer my condolences to the family. Secondly, I told him I was there to see if there was anything the Newark Police Department could do to help them. I offered my services. The guy, who was a well-known community organizer, told me to wait while he went back into the apartment. He came back out and invited me in. I went inside and talked to him. I let him know that since they were planning a march to protest Tasha's death and dignitaries like Al Sharpton and other local activists like Ras Baraka were going to be there, we'd like to help secure the march. We want to help you get through it without any problems. That was the least we could offer, so please let us know how we can help. The man thanked me for showing some kind of decency in offering help. Then he and Tasha's family said they'd let me know if we could help. Soon afterward I got a phone call saying yes, they'd like our help. Something like that wouldn't happen in a police department if you didn't have officers in there from groups like the Bronze Shields, officers who have that type of sensitivity toward the community. When I came back to the police department and told them the family said, "Yes we can help," all my supervisors were relieved like, "Thank you for doing that."

Labeeb Abdullah: When I became the Bronze Shields president, we'd get requests from the community—block watch groups—to come out and occupy the street corners where a lot of drug dealing was taking place. We'd get requests from all over Newark. We'd go out and shut down the drug operation, at least for a few hours. We did this every week. Afterward, we'd get a letter of thanks for coming out and patrolling. We'd go out sometimes with members of the Nation of Islam and patrol a neighborhood. People complained to us that they'd called the Newark Police Department, or they'd called Narcotics Squad for help and got no response. But the Bronze Shields would come out and do something. People said they were able to enjoy their evening without hearing gunshots. I took pride in the fact we were able to make some kind of difference. But it caused problems for us within the police department because we would do this patrolling on our own time. This was ironic because the department wanted us to be out there working with the community. Even within the Bronze Shields, some older members had a problem with that kind of community service. They would say, "You can go out there with Labeeb if you want to. But you're going to have problems. And if you get into trouble with the police department, we're not going to defend you." Not everybody was into the idea of patrolling the community. I felt some of them had brought into the idea of the us-versus-them type of policing.

Niles Wilson: When I was young, I remember the Bronze Shields patrolling in the community wearing their Bronze Shields jackets and helping out with different programs at school.

While the Bronze Shields's 1972 discrimination lawsuit is credited with increasing the number of Black officers in the Newark Police Department, the door was even slower in opening for women. That changed in 1981 when the department had its largest women recruitment class, a class that included trailblazing Bronze Shields members Barbara George and GiGi Foushee. As many of these new officers were African American, this changing face of the agency also meant a changing body for the Bronze Shields membership. Similar to the discrimination many Black male officers experienced in the 1950s and 1960s, women in the Bronze Shields also realized the battle they faced against discrimination on the force and in the organization.

Louis Greenleaf: There were always women in the Newark Police Department, but very, very few. You could count them on one hand. The department didn't go out of its way to recruit women. But that changed in the '80s when women started breaking the line.

Joseph Foushee: Following the lawsuit in the 1970s, a new wave of women recruits came in 1981, when eight black women and one Latina joined the force. GiGi Foushee, my wife, was one of them. She had a sister named Barbara George, who was on the force. There was also Mae Smith. The reason I'm aware of this is because they used to meet at my house, which became the headquarters for the females. These were some of the first female officers to work in the streets as police officers.

John L. Smith: Most of those Black female recruits became Bronze Shields.

Louis Greenleaf: Despite the Bronze Shields lawsuit in the '70s a lot of women still couldn't join the police department because they couldn't pass the physical exam.

Carrie Reed, Bronze Shields, NPD (1996-2015): I applied to the Newark Police Department a couple of times. I worked for the county, but then I got laid off. I took the written test for Newark again and passed. That was no problem. But I didn't pass the physical part of the exam. I'd only missed by about three seconds, supposedly. All the people monitoring the test were guys. You had to do something like run around a track six times in a certain amount of time. I was a former track runner, a sprinter. And I could run. There was a guy also taking the test. I ran past him twice during that test. I finished in 10 seconds. But the monitor timing me said I finished in 12 seconds. But the guy I ran past twice, the monitor said he finished in six seconds. That wasn't true. So I disputed it. Also, during the physical exam, the same recruit who I passed running was being introduced to the monitors by one of the officers. That happened before the exam. Like, let's say the recruit's name was Peter Smith. The officer was introducing the recruit to the monitors like, "Hey, this is Peter Smith. He's a long-time family friend." And they'd laugh and shake hands. I was shocked. How could they be introducing the recruits to the monitors? That's a no-no right there. But there was nothing you could do. I did what I was supposed to do in the right amount of time and still failed. The issue I had was that I finished in the same amount of time as some of the male recruits, but in the end, I failed while they passed. I said to myself we're going to have to do something about this. So I filed a complaint. I got a list from the Newark Police Department of all the women who didn't pass the test. And what I found was that some women failed the physical test by two or three seconds. After I saw that, I said somebody has got to hear this. This isn't right. Once I gathered the list of the women who failed the physical exam, I asked them if they wanted to file a class-action lawsuit. Only a few were interested, but many of them weren't. I filed a lawsuit. At the same time a few female police officers, who were already on the job, filed a lawsuit for discrimination. We eventually won the case, and they stopped using a stopwatch. The police department had to come up with a different way—a fair way—of testing physical fitness. But that change didn't just apply to Newark. It applied to all agencies of New Jersey Civil Services—corrections departments, sheriff departments, and even the fire department. That lawsuit further opened the door for women. The lawsuit helped get me on the force.

Mae Smith: When we came onto the force the male officers would tell us they didn't want to work with us. Put it this way, if I came onto the Newark Police Department now with what happened to me and other female officers back then, we'd all be millionaires. That lawsuit and the pay-out would have been epic. Female officers on the job today have advocates. But when I joined, we only had each other. There were nine of us and we met once every month. We turned it into a birthday club where we would talk about things. We did have some male police officers who were supportive. But most of them were not. To them, we had to prove ourselves.

John L. Smith: The increase of women on the job began to change the social dynamic of the police department. Back then, Christmas parties within the police department could get X-rated with strippers and other kinds of ladies. All the way live. After women started coming on the job, you couldn't do those types of things with lady police officers present. It wasn't decent.

Larry Brown: Our supervisors went around the locker room and told us we had to take down any pictures we had of women in our lockers, even though we didn't share the locker room with the women. But they had to find room to give them their own separate locker room. There may have been two women in each precinct, but they got private space. The guys were all crowded up in dirty, dingy locker rooms. That created a lot of animosity towards women on the job too.

Mae Smith: There was a woman who came on the force around the time I did, and she was pregnant. This officer worked at the 5th Precinct where they had her pumping gas while pregnant. A woman who worked for Gibson, named Helen De Mirette, saw this and was outraged. She went to the mayor and said, "How dare they allow a pregnant woman to pump gas." The next day the pregnant officer was put on a better detail.

Levi A. Holmes II: Men, to this day, still harbor negative feelings about women on the force. But back then it was heavy. Some men wouldn't work with women. If they were paired with a woman the man would call out sick.

Larry Brown: I had issues with working with a woman. I did not want to work under one in any circumstance. But for some reason, at one time I was partnered with a woman. I think this was supposed to be a punishment for something I did. I was partnered with Mae Smith. That was rough. I wouldn't let her drive. She had to go where I told her to go. And yes, what I did was mean and unfair. I can admit that. But what people also didn't know was, for me, it was about safety. I couldn't trust that a female would look out for me like the male partners I had. And when anything came over the radio, I always wanted to be the first one there. I was what you would call a hotdog or a street cop. I really liked the action. And everybody I worked with was the same way. If they weren't, we didn't work together. I got a different partner. That's the way it was. What changed me was one day Mae and I got a call, a stolen car call. We chased the stolen car and the thief bailed on us. I ran after one and Mae took off after the other. My guy got away. But Mae had hers. So we locked the guy up. After that I was impressed. Hell, she did better than me. Then there was another time, [we had] a domestic violence call. A husband and wife were fighting. We went there and broke it up. I was going to lock up the guy. I start putting him in the radio car and the guy started fighting me. Before you know it, he'd gotten the best of me. If Mae wasn't there no telling what might have happened. She yanked the guy off of me and saved me. That's what changed my mind.

Levi A. Holmes II: When I came on the job, I didn't understand how important women police officers were until I started seeing it. Before, the way the job was advertised made it seem this type of work wasn't for them. There was also the mentality that women can't stomach the job, and they didn't have the physical strength to do the job. But women bring a unique element. I see a lot of problems with male officers trying to defuse situations in public and it eventually turns into an ego-versus-ego or adrenaline-versus-adrenaline type of thing. If a female officer is there she will eventually defuse the situation without a conflict. No injuries and minimal arrests.

Sheilah Coley, Bronze Shields, NPD (1989-2014): I didn't personally experience anything horrible as far as sexism. But women were still a novelty when I joined. There were quite a few on the force but not a whole lot. I came from the military, so I was prepared for that. I didn't have many negative experiences as other women. I didn't have negative interactions with male partners. The biggest problem I encountered was bumping heads with leadership. That's because I always wanted to thoroughly know what they were having me do. If what they told me was contrary to what I should be doing, I spoke up. I'd even pull the police rulebook out to show them I was right.

Levi A. Holmes II: In my rookie year, there was a female police team in the South Ward, which is one of the most violent districts in the city. These women, a couple of whom were Bronze Shields, would take down the biggest drug dealers and gang members. It didn't make a difference. Those ladies handled their business. I would go to back them up and they'd ask me, "What are you doing here? We got this. We don't need you."

Mae Smith: Coming to folks as a member of the Bronze Shields they accepted me. One time there was a man who was wanted for a major drug bust. He was wanted, and they said he was extremely dangerous. He turned himself into me. I walked him through. I had another guy who escaped from the county jail and went to Bergen County. I was instrumental in bringing that person in. Afterwards, I received a "thank you" note from the Bergen County Police Department. The Caucasian officers got the spotlight for that capture, but it was okay because his family felt so trusting of me to turn their loved one in without him or anyone getting hurt. That meant a lot to me because it showed that the community thought enough of me.

Tijuana Burton, Bronze Shields, NPD (1989-2014): The women Bronze Shields were instrumental in my becoming an officer. When I applied for the job there was a physical exam. Somehow Mae Smith found out a small group of women were applying, and she reached out. She contacted me and said she was meeting in Branch Brook Park with the other ladies and if I was interested, to join them. She just wanted to give us an idea of what to expect during the physical exam. She also wanted us to be mentally prepared. I really appreciated the help because the Bronze Shields didn't have to do that. Once I finished the academy that's what made me want to join.

Anthony Kerr: There were quite a few women involved with the Bronze Shields. There were always women involved with the organization.

Mae Smith: I knew about the Bronze Shields before I joined the force. I joined because after I came on the force, people like Jeff Holloway and others came to us rookies and said you should become part of the organization. They told us about how the Bronze Shields had won a lawsuit, which made it easier for women and people of color to become police officers. So to me, it seemed like a great thing to be a part of.

Carrie Reed: I knew a lot about the Bronze Shields before I joined. I knew about a lot of the things they did for the community in the 1970s. I even attended a lot of these events, like the dances.

Mae Smith: There was a guy, a Black male officer, who said to me he didn't want us to become Bronze Shields. But once we became members, they accepted us. It wasn't a love fest at first. But we proved our worth and showed we could do the same job as them.

Shakoor Mustafa: Women in the Bronze Shields were and still are very protective of the organization. When I joined, they were like mothers so to speak. People won't outright say that, but that was the case.

Mae Smith: One of the best events when I was the vice president of the organization was the Christmas party. That was the chance for the community to see us outside of being the boogieman who were out to arrest people and lock them up. You were able to talk to them. We went to schools and talked, not as officers, but as Bronze Shields members.

Sheilah Coley: I met some of the women in the Bronze Shields like Barbara George and GiGi Foushee before joining. They told me about the struggles of women in the department. Then they invited me to an event where I heard how the Bronze Shields was started. After that, I wanted to be a part of it to continue the legacy. I wanted to fight for the rights of minority officers.

Thirty-four years after its birth, the Bronze Shields celebrated another milestone in 1993 when it elected Sheilah Coley as its first woman president. During her two terms, Sheilah signaled a new direction for the organization.

Joseph Foushee: Sheila Coley came behind after that 1981 wave of women recruits.

Sheilah Coley: From all the stories I heard about the early struggles and the fight for our rights, I felt like the Bronze Shields' leadership had become complacent. I joined the force in 1990. I ran for Bronze Shields president in 1992. When I ran one of the ladies told me they're never going to elect of female president. I said I'll just keep running until they do. I was defeated in 1992 but ran again in 1993. That time I won.

Levi A. Holmes II: When Sheilah ran a lot of people didn't want her to be the president. They said she hadn't been on the job long enough. She was a detective at the time. They felt she wasn't ready yet. So there was push-back. A lot of people stopped participating in the organization once she became the president.

Labeeb Abdullah: There was some controversy over Sheilah becoming Bronze Shields president, but not much. She'd come up through the ranks, and everybody knew her.

James Du Bose: Sheilah's two terms as president were wrought with opposition primarily because she was a woman. But she prevailed and ran the Bronze Shields successfully.

Bryan Morris: She was an excellent president. Smart woman. A no-nonsense person, she was not timid or intimidated by anyone.

Levi A. Holmes II: When Sheilah was the president it was all business. She is a no-nonsense type of person. She is very fact-based. In a male-dominated organization we may let facts slip by because we're all trying to be cool. Not with Sheilah. She'd say, "Where's the proof for your argument? Where's the reason? Where's the rationale?" If you didn't have your facts straight on what you wanted, she'd shut you down. But that's the person she's always been. She brought more of a business-conscious mentality to the Bronze Shields. She structured integrity back into the organization. She also stopped a lot of the nonsense that was going on. She brought some organization to our social club. She also changed the focus of the organization to advancing our members into higher positions within the department.

Sheilah Coley: To accomplish what I wanted to do with the Bronze Shields I saw we needed to have more productive meetings. Meetings are about conducting business. What I'd heard in most of the meeting was a lot of complaining. I made sure when we met there was an agenda that we followed. We laid out goals and what we wanted to achieve.

Gene Etchison: She advocated for women on the job. She made sure women took the promotional tests.

Sheilah Coley: If getting promotions were on our agenda, we'd have a meeting to figure out who was qualified. Then we'd hold promotional classes. Me and another member would volunteer on Saturdays and teach a promotional exam class for free. A big reason for the push during that time was while the police department reflected Newark's Black population, much of the department's management and leadership was white and male. Since I'd been on the force there wasn't one female supervisor. Barbara George eventually became the first female sergeant.

Tijuana Burton: Sheilah and I were a part of the same academy class. She was always driven. She didn't take no for an answer. Sheilah was very competitive. And she always excelled and tested very well. She was always the type of person that when the dust settled, she was always the one standing in the front of the line.

Sheilah Coley: I felt like we weren't pursuing new officers coming into the department. We weren't explaining to them the dos and don'ts of navigating the police department. I thought we should be more aggressive in going to the academy and talking to the incoming officers. We needed to explain to them that there is a blue line, but our struggle as Black police officers is not like the struggle of other officers on the force.

James Du Bose: During her two terms as president she helped re-open the Bronze Shields's headquarters. The building had been closed for some time. She oversaw the renovations of the first floor and she also got back the liquor license we'd lost twice under two previous presidents.

Gene Etchison: Sheilah saved our headquarters by taking out a mortgage on the building.

Levi A. Holmes II: Our social club helps us fund our various activities. People weren't paying attention to the details of the business. Sheilah brought more accountability to the business and made everybody responsible. She said we needed to be more about business and organizational structure.

John Scott-Bey: People didn't know where the money we generated—from liquor sales and dues—was going. People were asking what we were doing with the dues and money from the bar. During this time I was a little disgruntled with the Bronze Shields.

Shakoor Mustafa, Bronze Shields, NPD (1985-2010): I was in the Bronze Shields with Sheilah Coley. I remember during the month of Ramadan I asked one of the officers under her command to see if they could convince the Bronze Shields to give the Muslim officers a plaque in recognition of the holy month. Sheilah wasn't the Bronze Shields president yet. But when the officer asked the organization for something to recognize the Muslim officers, the person who was the president at that time said no. And I got mad. I said, "You take our dues and celebrate Christmas and give kids toys via a religious function." Although the president at the time wasn't budging on his decision, Sheilah stepped up. She said: "No. That's not right. We need to recognize the month of Ramadan." She did that. I thanked her and I said one day I thought she'd become a police director. She laughed.

Sheilah Coley: When the Bronze Shields started, they had a large presence in the community. We could go anywhere. We were expected to be everywhere. There was a high expectation from the people. For the most part, we did our best to deliver. But with changes in leadership and philosophies over the years, our priorities shifted. Whenever we came to the Bronze Shields's headquarters, we always left our rank at the door. We were just one organization. As time went on there were people who wanted to use their police rank in the organization. As a result, you weren't getting a true consensus on what the Bronze Shields should be doing. That's because people became afraid to speak up. They didn't know what was going to happen to them once they left the meeting. They might get punished for being honest. That became an issue.

Labeeb Abdullah: As president Sheilah helped to increase our membership. We got involved in issues. We were asked to come to the governor's mansion to participate in workshops regarding community policing. This was around the time when racial profiling was first becoming a national issue in the news.

Sheilah Coley: I had a very supportive group. They came out and helped me get things done. We became more active in the community, which I thought was another area that had dwindled when I joined the Bronze Shields. We looked at ways to grow the Shields because now the organization was about more than just getting Black officers hired. That wasn't a problem. After the 1974 consent decree following our lawsuit, the Newark Police Department reflected the city's predominantly Black population. Now we had to retain the Black officers and make sure they advanced.

Despite the work the Bronze Shields did over the years to make Black cops a positive force among Newark residence, the 1997 police shooting of Dannette "Strawberry" Daniels revealed a renewed rift between cops and the community. The shooting almost proved as explosive as the 1967 rebellion. Like numerous cities across America, Newark residence were caught between living with rising, rampant violent crime and drugs and the increasingly aggressive policing meant to deal with it. Not to mention this was four years following the Los Angeles riots, which made police brutality a hot topic within Black America. With the shock of the Daniels shooting, members of the Bronze Shields worked to help the city avoid a repeat of '67 by attempting to meet outrage with understanding and compassion.

Sheilah Coley: I started working in Internal Affairs during this time. That was my first Internal Affairs investigation. I was in training when I got dispatched to this police shooting in the South Ward.

Bryan Morris: That was the police shooting of Dannette "Strawberry" Daniels by Officer Robert "Bobby" Leaks, Jr. on Clinton and Chadwick Avenues. What happened was the police were riding through Chadwick and Bergen, which was a known drug area. A group called the Zoo Crew was big there. Bobby Leaks, his partner, and some other officers went up there and made a drug arrest. Strawberry Daniels, who was involved in the drug industry in some form, was arrested and put in the back of an unmarked police car. Because it was unmarked, the car didn't have a screen blocking off the front seat from the back seat. Strawberry slipped out of the handcuffs, jumped into the driver's seat, and put the car in drive. She actually started driving in reverse. Bobby, who was outside the vehicle, opened the car door and tried to make her stop. But the woman kept driving, and he was being dragged down the street. I don't remember if he was in the car window or the door but she was going backwards. And she wouldn't stop. So he pulled his gun out and shot her.

Anthony Kerr: When they arrested Strawberry Williams, they also arrested a teenage boy who was just sitting on the corner. People were mad. It was damn near a riot even before the shooting. When they put Strawberry in the unmarked car, guys on the corner started antagonizing the police. By this time, all the officers were out of their cars. Since the situation was becoming combative, they couldn't return to their vehicles. While they were preoccupied with the crowd, Strawberry Williams got in the front seat of the unmarked cop car and started to take off. The whole crowd looked at the incident as, "Wow, the cop just shot and killed her." They were all in shock.

Sheilah Coley: I tried to figure out exactly what happened as I was trying to keep the crowd back. We also had to call additional officers because the situation was almost at riot stage. When I tried to get in my car, it wouldn't start. I had to leave my car there and catch a ride to the South Ward precinct, which was a couple of blocks away. At the precinct, we gathered our notes as to what happened. I fully disclosed that Bobby Leaks and I used to patrol together in the West District, to which I was told I couldn't do the investigation. I promised I could be impartial, but then I realized that no matter what the outcome was, even if it comes from me, it's not going to help with the anger that was building up outside in the street. With that said I was off the case.

John Scott-Bey: As a lieutenant they made me stand out on Clinton Avenue all summer long with that situation. It was because one of my officers, who was a Muslim, arrested that 16-year old boy. Basically he was arrested because he'd refused to get off the corner. I told the officer he had to watch what he did because he could incite a crowd, which is exactly what happened. Shortly afterward people from the community, who were pissed about the shooting, came to the precinct and questioned why we arrested the kid. Since I was a lieutenant I told the crowd, "Hey, I'm not going to let anything happen to the boy. I'll bring him back as soon as they finish record-checking him." When my captain came back to the precinct, he saw the boy was gone. I explained that I took the boy back to the corner, which is what I'd promised those people I'd do.

Anthony Kerr: Once the city locked down Clinton Avenue and put a curfew in effect, a group of us Muslim officers most of whom were Bronze Shields, went to the area to keep the peace. We had to do that because the city was about to use force. After the shooting, while people expressed their anger, the police department wanted to send an Emergency Response Team (E.R.T.) to deal with the Zoo Crew. They were the main group leading the protest against the shooting. They were speaking out against brutality. During the curfew the E.R.T. was on standby in case a riot broke out. Me and a group of Muslim officers, which included Shakoor Mustafa and Labeeb Abdullah, all went into the community and talked to people. I'm from the area, so I knew the lay of the land. Also, in the Black community, Muslims aren't seen as a threat. We're trusted. We went in there and talked to the few brothers who were stirring the crowds up. We told them, "You don't know what you're up against. The police are going to come in here with a show of force. So if you're going to speak then speak. But don't stir up violence." That's what our mission was. We wanted to go in there and keep things cool.

Derrick Hatcher: The community was outraged. Strawberry was an individual who everyone in that area knew. That incident was a tipping point because that was an area where people sold a lot of drugs. It was a neighborhood that needed to be heavily policed. So it became a flashpoint in the relationship between the community and the police because they didn't like any type of police presence there because of the illegal activity. After the shooting you had the community—homeowners, activists, and even those involved in the illegal activities—marching on City Hall.

Sheilah Coley: A large crowd gathered very quickly. They were yelling about police brutality. The protest was being led by Ras Baraka. He wasn't in politics at the time. He was a community activist. He led people with the notion that they shouldn't stand for police shootings anymore. He thought it was an abuse of power. The rumors that were circulating about the case at the time didn't help either.

Labeeb Abdullah, Bronze Shields, NPD (1991-Present): This was a few years after the Rodney King beating and the L.A. riots. So people were very conscious of police brutality. Also, around the country, you had the popularity of the rap group N.W.A, who had a song called "Fuck Tha Police." That was the sentiment among a lot of people. In Newark, we had our own issues, but that was the state of affairs.

John Scott-Bey: During that time they had intelligence officers out there watching the protest. Mae Smith was one of the people watching the marches.

Mae Smith: We just had to keep an eye on things when the marches and protests started. Me and Paul Braswell became part of the protests. We were gathering intelligence. We had to make sure there wasn't going to be any rioting. And there wasn't. But there was enough noise to make the police department see what was going on. The march went from Bergen Street to City Hall. There were members of the Zoo Crew, which was organizing the march, who recognized Paul and I as officers. But they never said anything. Ras Baraka saw us there too. He recognized us but didn't say anything. And if anything happened at the march, they could easily say two officers in attendance were keeping an eye on things. It was a peaceful march, but we had to write down whatever was said. We just blended in and took notes. Some called what we did infiltrating, but we had to know what was happening.

John Scott-Bey: Before the group marched on City Hall, Amiri Baraka, Ras's father, was handing out flyers about police brutality.

Bryan Morris: Ras organized the main rallies in the area. He staged a protest march down Clinton Avenue to City Hall. That march was the beginning of his political career. He may have run for mayor before then. But those marches put him in the spotlight.

Anthony Kerr: That protest helped light Ras's political path within

Newark. He was outspoken. At that time many officers thought he was anti-police because he wasn't quiet about what happened. He was vocal about advocating for the community.

Levi A. Holmes II: I think that was the moment Ras saw that you could have only minimal impact as a community activist if you are trying to make changes in the city. Participating in the conversation, while having a seat at the political bargaining table, gives you more leverage. He'd see that later on in his career as mayor. Before then, everyone knew who he was. He was a lightning rod. When he spoke everyone listened.

Labeeb Abdullah: Ras Baraka only protested and marched for what was right. I admired him. He had enough courage to go on the frontline when he had no power. He had the desire to do what was right.

Mae Smith: The people protesting wanted to make sure the police officers involved with the shooting would be tried in court. The people also wanted answers as to what happened. They wanted the truth. They didn't want any cover-ups. They needed answers. I'm just glad nothing serious happened afterwards. I was a police officer. But more than that I was a Black woman who lived in Newark. I was also affected by what went on in the community.

Levi A. Holmes II: The shooting also put Sharpe James at odds with the police. During that time, a certain segment of the police turned their backs when Sharpe spoke to them. There was a large rally at City Hall after the incident, and the mayor disagreed with the police department's position. They felt they acted properly after the shooting. But Sharpe thought they acted improperly. There were a little over 100 officers there when Sharpe spoke. When he began talking about the incident, all the officers turned their backs. That move was led by the F.O.P. Sharpe was furious after that.

Tijuana Burton: The unions got together and had us turn our back on the mayor. The F.O.P. was galvanizing us like it was an "us" against "them" thing. Don't get me wrong. Everybody loved Sharpe James. But it appeared to the union that he was picking a side and chastising the police like we did something wrong. All we were doing was doing our job. So it was like daddy picking sides. Before the rally, we were told to turn our backs. I remember us being in uniform and standing outside and doing just that. It was like he'd turned on us, so we were giving him a taste of his own medicine.

Gene Etchison: Sharpe James was pissed off at that shooting. He used to be the councilman for that district. He was shocked that we would do such a thing. No shooting like that had ever occurred in Newark. People were shocked. But it wasn't about Sharpe. It was about this officer who had a clean record, was forced into a situation, and had to act. Bobby Leaks was a great guy. He wouldn't hurt anyone. He was also a stand-up cop. But they put him through the ringer.

Derrick Hatcher: We only did that because we wanted Sharpe James not to suspend Bobby. We wanted Sharpe to allow him to work and take care of his family. The shooting was justified. But he was suspended, and the matter went to a grand jury. Sharpe had given in to the chants of the community. But in the end, Bobby Leaks was found innocent.

In 1998, two Bronze Shields members took a stand for religious rights that made national headlines. Shakoor Mustafa, who'd been on the force for 12 years and Farooq Abdul-Aziz, who'd been an officer for nine years, were both devout Sunni Muslims. Both faced dismissal from the Newark Police Department for wearing beards, which are a part of their religion. Under a 1971 police department regulation requiring all officers to be clean-shaven, Mustafa and Abdul-Aziz were ordered to cut their facial hair. Feeling their First Amendment rights were being violated, the two officers challenged the Newark Police Department. The outcome of the trial would set a new precedence for religious freedom amongst workers nationwide.

Shakoor Mustafa: During a certain time Muslim officers felt like they were being persecuted. Ironically, we had a Black police administration. We went up against a Black administration because they were denying us our religious rights.

James Du Bose: Newark's chief of police Thomas C. O'Reilly announced a zero-tolerance policy for officers who would not comply with the no-beards rule. Back then you needed medical clearance to wear a beard. But we had quite a few officers who were Muslim. And the beard is a part of their belief system.

Shakoor Mustafa: This began with an exchange between Mayor Sharpe James and me. I used to be on his security detail before we had a disagreement. One day I'm going out to get something to eat and Mayor James sees me going to the store. He stops me and asks, "They let you wear that beard on the job?" I told him, "Just because I'm an officer I can't lose who I am as a Muslim." He said, "Okay." After that, he called William Celester, who was the police director then, and shouted, "Who's running the goddamn police department!? You have a guy on duty with a beard as long as Santa Claus!" Celester asked who the officer was, and the Mayor said it was me. Celester explained that I'd always had that beard. Mayor James told Celester either he terminate me from the job or he—the mayor—will get someone who can do it. So the police director sent word to the captain that I have to answer the question: "Why do I wear a beard?"

Joseph Foushee: I saw Shakoor's transformation as an officer into what he became. Around that time, my age kicked in and I didn't understand his fight. He became this orthodox Muslim, and I didn't understand the importance of what was going on or what he was trying to achieve. I've since come to understand. But back then, while he was going through it—having been taken off of

Mayor James's security detail shortly before—I didn't understand. But from what I could see, Shakoor was too bright to be Sharpe's bodyguard because to do that job and be successful, you have to be a non-person. And a person like Shakoor has too much intelligence. It's not that Sharpe was anti-intelligent but he's the kind of guy that will say, "I'm going to stick this guy in the back, but you're going to swear that I didn't do it." And if you said okay, you could be with him. But if you say, "No, I'm telling the truth," then you can't be with him. I think I was the guy who put Shakoor on that detail. When I thought of people for the job, I picked the brightest, articulate people who would put the police department's best foot forward.

Shakoor Mustafa: I was taken off Sharpe's security detail because of a disagreement while on a trip in Atlanta. I was guarding him when he went to visit a strip club. He tells me, "Go put $20 on that girl right there." He caught me off-guard with that one. I asked him who he was talking to. He was shocked at my response. He really expected me to join in the strip club activities. I told him I didn't come on the job looking for leadership. I already have that. He said, "Okay. When we get back to Newark let me have my gold badge back." The gold badge is given to detectives. I told him, "That's why I took the civil service exam. I don't have to be anyone's flunky." After that, the mayor thought I was an up-start, a troublemaker. But I felt offended that he would even ask me to compromise who I am. When we came back to Newark, I contacted Claude Coleman who was the police director at that time. I told him I couldn't work with the mayor anymore. He's not looking for security. He's looking for a flunky. Claude told me, "Listen, I'm trying to put people around the mayor who can think for themselves." Then he asked me to be patient. But it was too late. Shortly afterward, the Mayor asked that I be put back on patrol in the cellblock to watch prisoners. Then the beard issue came up.

Anthony Kerr: At first the police department allowed the full beard. Then they switched and said no, we're not going to let you wear it. That's where it originally started. One of the police captains also saw a bunch of narcotics officers who didn't wear uniforms. Some of them had beards and some of them didn't have beards. They were all at a parade. Well, the captain made a big issue about it and demanded that everybody cut their beards while on duty or be terminated from their positions. Everybody with beards was like, "We can't cut our beards." When that order came down, I was wearing a beard at that time and I refused to cut it. Shakoor and Farooq fought against this rule through the F.O.P. while Kevin Rhodes and I fought with the backing of the Equal Employment Opportunity Commission (E.E.O.C.). But we all eventually filed a discrimination suit.

Labeeb Abdullah: I wasn't a part of the lawsuit, but I do remember my debates about facial hair in the police department. One time when I was teaching at the police academy, I had a conversation with the then police director that turned into a slight argument. People within the department were saying you don't need to wear a beard. But we made it clear that we stood with the Muslim officers for their religious rights. We were there as the Bronze Shields [members], too. We made that publicly known. The police director didn't think that was right. He still didn't think we should be able to wear our beards. He said, "Farrakhan's a Muslim and he doesn't have a beard." And I responded, "And you don't like him. So why are you using him as a litmus test?"

Shakoor Mustafa: Once word got out that a battle was brewing between me and the administration over my beard, people started trying to convince me to stop. They were saying, "You're making a $100,000 a year for doing easy work. Why keep the beard?" I told them if I wasn't a practicing Muslim, I wouldn't wear a beard." I wouldn't wear it because personally, it makes you look older and takes away my youth. But if they were going to fire me over this, the one who's commanding me to wear the beard—Allah—is going to be responsible for me.

Anthony Kerr: We forged ahead anyway. We were staying true to our religion. That's what was important.

Bryan Morris: We were absolutely supportive. There were many Muslims on the job by then. The beard is a sign of a man in Islamic culture—the more powerful the beard, the more powerful the man.

Anthony Kerr: It was four of us initially involved in that. It was me, Shakoor Mustafa, Kevin Rhodes and Farooq Abdul-Aziz. At first it was four of us. But in the end, it grew to 12 of us. The case was fought from two sides. Farooq and Mustafa fought with the help of the F.O.P., using the rules and regulations to fight the city.

Shakoor Mustafa: My friend Farooq Abdul-Aziz went to the F.O.P. and told them, "The administration is persecuting us. We pay your dues and you're doing nothing about this." After they told him to calm down, they said they'd provide us with an attorney. I thought the attorney they hired for us was a little too young for the job. At first, I thought the union was trying to placate us with someone who didn't know what he was doing, and we'd lose. I was wrong. We went to federal court and the judge heard both sides. Our side was arguing that we're being persecuted for wearing beards while the other side said no one was being persecuted.

Carrie Reed: They knew I was one of the people who would stand with them. Shakoor always kept me updated on what was going on with his case.

Shakoor Mustafa: During the trial the judge says he'd heard enough. Then he awarded us the right to wear beards. The courtroom erupted with cheers. I was crying. A lot of Muslims and attorneys came to that trial because it was poised to set a new precedent for religious freedom. And it did. The impact of that ruling was far-reaching. Since that time other cases in other states and cities went to trial regarding religious rights. And not just for Muslims, but for Christians and Orthodox Jews and other beliefs.

Anthony Kerr: The litigation of the case forced the lawsuit into federal court. And we won. Sharpe James didn't like the fact that we won. The city appealed the suit, and we won again.

Shakoor Mustafa: The Bronze Shields was the organization that came into the courtroom and supported me. The F.O.P. paid for the attorney. But the Bronze Shields came in to make the administration responsible and also show their allegiance to us. I really appreciated that.

Gene Etchison: I sat in on that court hearing when they won. I was president of the Bronze Shields during that time. Most of the plaintiffs were Bronze Shields members. Some people in the department warned me not to go and get involved. I said no, they are members. Many members came in civilian clothes, but they were there to support and watch them win. Their win opened things up for Muslims statewide. That's why you see officers throughout the state wearing beards. Lawsuits like that didn't just affect Newark. They affected the state because others filed similar lawsuits and used that outcome to plead their case. That victory set a new precedence.

Shakoor Mustafa: Years later I ran into Sharpe James again. While on duty I went into a store to buy something. Sharpe was in the store. This was years later around the time he'd been indicted. He saw me when I came in and he said, "Aaaah, you mad with me?" He was talking about our disagreement. I said, "What am I mad at you about?" I ultimately won my case. They awarded me a financial reward. I said to Sharpe, "I've got a brand new Audi that the city provided for me. And I'm still on the job. I never lost a day. What am I mad at?" He said, "Well, it looks like I might be going to jail." I said, "It's just like Malcolm X said, it's 'the chickens coming home to roost.' When you lay down with dogs, you come up with fleas." But, beyond that, I've always had a candid relationship with Sharpe James. No animosity or malice between us. And I'd like to think that when we see each other, he's frank with me. One time I was working security at Beth Israel Hospital and Sharpe had been admitted for heart issues. Someone told me he'd come in, and when I got off work that morning I went to his room to see him.

The March 8, 1998 issue of Jet *magazine marked another historic moment for the Newark Police Department when Barbara George, a prominent Bronze Shields member, was sworn in as the city's first female police captain by Mayor Sharpe James. Before her promotion, George had commanded the Newark Police Department's rape unit called SARA (Sexual Assault Rape Analysis) where she was credited with improving the unit's efficiency.*

Tijuana Burton: That was a big deal. Law enforcement is male-driven, and you have to deal with preconceived notions about women police officers. They aren't tough enough for the job. It's a man's job. Barbara moving up the ranks like that and becoming a captain dispelled all those myths. It was inspiring. It told women we had a place here and we can make a difference.

Sheilah Coley: There was some talk saying that Barbara hadn't done enough to earn the promotion. Whenever I heard those comments, I would ask the person what made Barbara less qualified than some male captain—I'd name someone we both knew wasn't a good leader. What made Barbra different or less worthy than them? When the person couldn't answer my question, I'd inform them that the only difference I saw was that Barbara's a Black woman. They needed to get over that.

Levi A. Holmes II: Barbara George was a role model for women in the department and officers in general. She stood her ground regardless of who liked her and who didn't. She learned the laws. She knew what she was talking about, and she would take anybody to task. She wasn't the most personable individual. But those who understood the impact of her promotion were very happy for her.

Gene Etchison: She was the head of the Sexual Assault Rape

Analysis unit (SARA) before she became Captain. She turned that unit around and improved it quickly. She was misunderstood because she was hard on folks. But she gave you the hard love and facts. She'd tell you what you needed to do and what you don't do. She gave a lot of women hope, especially if they were trying to move up in rank. She did that for Sheilah Coley and many other women who advanced in the department.

Sheilah Coley: She was the captain of the trial board. There were always complaints about inequities regarding Black officers getting disciplined versus white officers. Her job was to make sure that the discipline the officers received fit the charges they were brought up on. Basically she made sure officers weren't overly punished for small offenses, a trend that seemed to plague Black officers but not white ones.

John L. Smith: She was very smart and ambitious and it showed because she rose through the department quickly. She was a Bronze Shields member. She wasn't very active politically. She was the laid-back type.

Mae Smith: We graduated from the police academy together. I knew her family since I was a teenager. What made me proud was that any position she obtained she truly deserved it because she worked harder than any man to get it. She earned her title and I always honored that. If she was sergeant, I addressed her as such—not Barbara, because she earned the respect. That was especially the case when she became captain. We females were very supportive of Barbara. Had she not passed away a few years later she would have made police director. That's how great she was. She knew everything from A to Z about the job. Some people thought she was hard on those who worked for her. If you handed in a half-ass report, she'd make you do it over and do it right. She made people into good police officers.

Sheilah Coley: We knew that her becoming captain had to

happen. It's easy for women to get lost in the shuffle. So we knew we had to support her and make her successful in order for us to move up. After that a few of us were promoted. But to show how long a process this was, when I eventually made sergeant, I was the third woman to achieve that in the history of the Newark Police Department. Mind you, the department was established in 1857. That showed you how women weren't being allowed to keep up with their male counterparts.

Floyd Bostic Jr., co-founder and first president of the Bronze Shields. (*Courtesy of the family of Floyd Bostic Jr.*)

Early members and co-founders. (*Top row L to R*) Floyd Bostic Jr., Theodore Howard. (*Middle row L-R*) Horace Braswell, Charles E. Harris, Donald G. Harper. (*Bottom row L to R*) Bobie Cottle, Charles I'Gus, Walter M. Davis (*Courtesy of the family of Floyd Bostic Jr.*)

Shortly after Hugh J. Addonizio became Newark's mayor in 1962, police director Dominick A. Spina (bottom row, third from the left), in a historic move, promoted 10 Black police officers to detective. Many of them were Bronze Shields, including Floyd Bostic Jr. (top left), Horace Braswell (Bottom row, first on the right) and Bobie Cotttle. (*Courtesy of the family of Floyd Bostic Jr.*)

Bronze Shields co-founder, Edward Williams, became Newark's first African American police captain in 1968. (*Courtesy of the family of Floyd Bostic Jr.*)

Edward Kerr was Newark's first Black police director from 1972 to 1974. (*Courtesy of Anthony Kerr*)

Hubert Williams, one of the Bronze Shields "young turks," was Newark's police director from 1974 to 1985. (*Courtesy of the family of Floyd Bostic Jr.*)

The women of the Bronze Shields after graduating from the police academy in 1981—a part of the largest group of female recruits at the time. (*L to R*) Barbara George (who would become Newark's first woman police captain), GiGi Foushee, Marion Simmons, Benita Johnson, Mae Smith and Mayor Kenneth A. Gibson. (*Courtesy of the family of Floyd Bostic Jr.*)

The former Bronze Shields headquarter at 43 William Street in downtown Newark. Leonard McGhee and Calvin Larkins helped purchase the property in 1983. (*Courtesy of Newark Bronze Shields*)

The first woman president of the Bronze Shields, Shielah Coley, in 1993. Coley also became Newark's first female police chief and, later, police director. (*Courtesy of Sheilah Coley*)

The Bronze Shields basketball team, while helping raise money for a number of community-based charities, helped bridge alliances between Newark police and Black residents. Pictured left to right: Carl Cobb, Fred Davis and Phil Davis. (*Courtesy of Newark Bronze Shields*)

Shakoor Mustafa, a Bronze Shields member and a Sunni Muslim, was part of a historic lawsuit claiming religious discrimination within the Newark Police Department. (*Courtesy of Shakoor Mustafa*)

Anthony Kerr, son of former Newark police director Edward Kerr, also filed a complaint against NPD for not allowing Muslim officers to wear beards for religious reasons. (*Courtesy of Anthony Kerr*)

Former Bronze Shields president, Ronald Glover, is credited with sparking the resurgence of the Bronze Shields in the 21st Century. (*Courtesy of Ronald Glover*)

Levi A. Holmes II, a former Bronze Shields president, helped revitalize the organization's prominence within Newark politics and community service. (*Courtesy of Levi A. Homes II*)

Chapter 6

NEWARK'S NEW BREED (1999-2008)

Heading into the 21st Century, the Bronze Shields was on the verge of celebrating its 50th anniversary. The organization's goal of fighting for racial equality within the Newark Police Department was several decades in the past. And like many civil rights organizations that pushed for inclusion and recognition, there comes a period where once a seat at the table has been obtained, lethargy, contentment and hubris sets in. The Bronze Shields were no different. The Newark Police Department had become a true reflection of the city's population. African Americans comprised 38 percent of the force, Latinos made up 35 percent and whites were 27 percent. Talk to Bronze Shields members from any era and they will tell you that after the organization helped improve the treatment and career path of Black officers, it suffered a noticeable identity crisis. Was the Bronze Shields still fighting for the civil rights of Black police officers? Was it a social club? How would it engage the community, or would it engage the community at all? How will the Bronze Shields redefine themselves? And who would be the person to re-set and redefine the Bronze Shields's mission and identity?

After a lengthy dry season heading into the 2000s, the answer came from within the ranks of a new generation of Black cops.

Ronald Glover, Bronze Shields, NPD (1994-2002): Upon learning about the Bronze Shields's history I thought it was exciting, especially seeing how they opened doors in the police department. I thought they were heroic and powerful. But once I became an active member, I saw the organization had lost a bit of that fire and needed a lot of work bringing it back. There was a legacy the Bronze Shields wasn't living up to.

Bryan Morris: I don't think there was a time when the Bronze Shields wasn't relevant. I don't think it lost relevancy. But the organization wasn't as recognized by the political entities of the city at a certain time.

Niles Wilson: Long-time organizations always go through a period where younger people question the need to be a part of the group. The older guys were trying to ensure the legacy of the Bronze Shields continued with a new crop of police officers.

Levi A. Holmes II: After Ken Gibson was elected mayor, the organization was at its apex. It was 100 percent involved in both politics and the community. As time went on, participation started to wane.

Tijuana Burton: When I first joined the Shields, they were very active in the community. After all, they reached out to me. That's why I wanted to join. At some point, it wasn't that active anymore. They still had their annual party. But the organization just seemed to be more about that than it was about the community.

Levi A. Holmes II: I heard stories about how during the 1967 rebellion, people asked for the Bronze Shields. They didn't want to talk to an officer unless that officer was a Bronze Shields. By the time I joined in the 1990s we no longer had that impact. When I joined there were people on the city council saying we didn't do much. They even said we weren't relevant anymore.

Charles Upshaw Jr. Bronze Shields, NPD (1981-1999): It started to feel like a fledgling organization with a fledgling membership. It wasn't being well supported. When I would go to meetings there would only be a handful of people. I was a part of the honor guard, which performed during the Black Heritage Parade. We had a traveling basketball team. Outside of that, the biggest part of being in the Bronze Shields was getting substantial positions within the police department. It became more of a political arm of the Newark Police Department. It also, for the most part, had become a social organization about social activities. There was nothing substantial going on.

Levi A. Holmes II: We didn't have control of the membership. We had males and females in the organization. But sometimes, things would get out of hand if a male and a female disagreed. It was to the point where a civil disagreement would almost turn into a fistfight in the meeting.

Anthony Kerr: There was the annual toy drive around Christmas time. The kids came down to our building. That probably was the only consistent thing we did. There may have been a turkey giveaway for Thanksgiving. But for the most part, most of our community activities had been abandoned. And remember, the people used to look to the Bronze Shields for activities. So when people can't look to you for that, you become persona non grata.

Charles Upshaw Jr.: In the late 1990s the Bronze Shields began to lose some of their steam. Part of the reason was that our membership wasn't that active. We also weren't getting a lot of members within the recruit classes coming in. Many of the older guys weren't doing what they needed to bring in younger members. Nor did they help groom younger members to take the reins of the organization. To me, it seemed people were just concerned with maintaining control of the Bronze Shields. We'd also lost touch with the community. We'd become known for showing up to parades and funerals.

Levi A. Holmes II: The Bronze Shields were actively doing things in the city. But they also lacked the organization structure I thought they should have had. That's why I spent time with the presidents: to see who was taking the Bronze Shields to the next level.

Gene Etchison: People started asking, "What do I get out of it?" And as that was happening, the organization for Latino officers, the Hispanic Law Enforcement Society, began to grow. I guess the leadership of the Bronze Shields started to recognize that and felt the Bronze Shields needed to get back in the community. We had lost track of that in the late 1990s. It was a brief period where people were becoming too cautious about their stances in the department. The leadership was afraid of ruffling feathers and jeopardizing their positions. But old heads like Leonard McGhee and others began speaking up. They would say, "People come to us for help. Don't let this organization die out."

Tijuana Burton: This was around the time when the Hispanic Law Enforcement Society, the Latino police organization, was on the rise. This was in the late '90s or early 2000s. That organization was getting active. Their membership was growing, and their presence was strong in the Latino community. They were united and cohesive. When promotion time came around, they were organizing study groups to help their members. They were heavily recruiting in their neighborhoods. If an officer got in trouble, they would rally around him or her with support. They were thriving. I didn't see that so much with the Bronze Shields. I don't know if it had to do with changing leadership, but the organization just wasn't as active or cohesive.

Anthony Kerr: The Bronze Shields's leadership, during that time, didn't want to get involved with someone else's problems and in turn, jeopardize their position in the police department. If they liked you or you were cool with someone, then they might make a phone call for you and straighten things out. But that wasn't happening often enough. There was a noticeable disconnect within the Bronze Shields. You had the haves and the have-nots. It wasn't blatantly obvious. But you knew it was there. As time went on, the have-nots began to see no reason to be in the Bronze Shields. As an officer, you're already a part of a fraternal police organization via the union who would fight for you within the police department. So why should I be a Bronze Shields member? They take money out of your check and there'd be no benefit. When you got cops on the street questioning your validity, that's going to trickle down to new recruits who won't see a need to join.

Leonard McGhee: During that time, the Bronze Shields was just about surviving. The social club was what kept the Bronze Shields alive. That and the payroll deduction brought in funds. Things were running administratively. Basically, by the mid to late 1990s, the Bronze Shields operated as a social club. But then again, by that time things weren't like they used to be in the old days. The disturbances and the disorder between the Black community and the police department had pretty much died down. And the need wasn't there as much as it was.

Anthony Kerr: The Bronze Shields still had power. But that power had shifted toward the political side. Its presence in the community diminished, which honestly also lessened our political power. If you're a part of the community, then the politicians see you as powerful. However, if you stop doing things in the community your political power decreases. If you stop beating your drum in the community and saying, "We're the Bronze Shields," you lose touch.

Bryan Morris: When I was president I was not politically connected. I thought I was a good president. But the organization wasn't as lively as it was. The survival issue had to do with how the organization was viewed. If political connections are what allows an organization to survive it will thrive. But that's only if politicians see it as a viable force or a useful tool for their agenda. If they don't see you as a force capable of pushing their agenda, you won't remain vital. You might not even be able to do things in the community because the political powers won't allow that to happen. So the organization did suffer and diminish in power over a 10-year period.

Anthony Kerr: Your political clout is reduced when you stop taking stances on different things. As a result, you become just another fraternal organization. So when I joined, the name was still strong but we mattered less. The Bronze Shields was more fraternal. A lot of the members who were trustees were mainly concerned with reaping the benefits of being Bronze Shields members—getting good details, getting good positions—while everybody else was left to fend for themselves.

Labeeb Abdullah: Some of the younger officers disassociated from it. There were also some unrealistic expectations of the organization. People didn't want to be active or participate in any capacity but then expected to get support when they got into a bad situation. Sometimes it wasn't that we didn't want to support them. It was just a matter of a situation where nothing could be done to help them. An organization is no better than its members.

Anthony Kerr: As an organization, you have your social strengths. You also have your political and fraternal strengths. Since the Bronze Shields had stopped being so social, everything became about gaining positions or maintaining a position on the job. No one wanted to make waves or piss off the political power structure. But the flip side was, the only way to keep politicians in check was around election time. During the rest of the time you don't see them get anything done until it was time to get your vote. But if an organization has a strong social base you can push the political leadership to act in your favor. The people who ran the Bronze Shields, who had administrative jobs, weren't stepping up. If an officer had a problem within the department, the Bronze Shields leadership did not come to his or her defense. The young officers started to see this right away. And they began to feel they couldn't count on the organization. They were starting to say things like, "Look, man, you're willing to take my dues out of my salary, but you won't help me when I need help." As a result, our membership declined. It declined quite a bit from the '90s into the 2000s. It was a slow but steady decline. It became like an old Jedi Knight that didn't seem to exist anymore. It just faded into the background.

Shakoor Mustafa: My initial thoughts upon joining were that the Bronze Shields was too beholden to its legacy. They'd expected people to pay homage to them because of their legacy. I didn't know the Bronze Shields, so I was a bit stand-offish when I joined. I didn't think they were going in the right direction. I thought they should be concentrating on what vision the new members were bringing to the table. Look to the future instead of the past.

Niles Wilson: What I experienced was more of what the older guys were saying to the younger ones: "Hey, young buck, open your eyes. We've been through a few battles and paved the way for you. Don't just drop the organization and think you don't need it. You need it, you just don't know it yet." That's how I saw the issue of the Bronze Shields. But looking back when I was a new recruit, we were excited to be on the job but we also had other dreams and other goals. Unless you were a second-generation cop, where you're following your dad's footsteps, you didn't really understand the internal problems and racial issues within the police department. You had no idea. The older guys were trying to mentor us. But when you're young you think you have all the answers. That's until you get in and see maneuvering within this job is more complicated than you thought. Then you're like, "Hold on. Wait a minute. I'm in trouble and I need some help." The older guys were saying, this is what we are here for. You need this organization.

Mae Smith: We had younger people joining the Newark Police Department who had degrees. I expected them to do well on the promotional exams because of their education. But some of them had forgotten that it's more than just passing that test. Back when I joined the Newark Police Department, the Black police officers were more tightknit despite how they felt about us female officers. But during a certain time you'd have officers who felt there was no need for the Bronze Shields. It's kind of like how some people say there's no longer a need for the NAACP. You had to argue tooth and nail to get young Black officers to join the Shields because they felt they didn't need it. I know things have changed but you still have to respect the old. But at the same time, the old guys have to respect new ways.

Labeeb Abdullah: There were always accomplishments. I supported the organization if they were doing something. But I kind of pulled back from the Shields. The state of the organization was kind of dismal. The unfortunate thing was that the politics of the day would spill over into the organization.

Mae Smith: Some people might say, "Well, the things you accomplished were back then. This is now." Those people don't understand that "now" wouldn't exist if it wasn't for those people that did something then. I always ask young officers, "What have you done for the Bronze Shields?" It's because of them that you have a job.

Gene Etchison: Also, a lot of people were retiring from the police department. As that was happening, the younger Black officers began to feel they were entitled to everything. They didn't understanding that, as a Black person, you have to fight and keep fighting to get what you want to make things better for the person coming behind you. There was no urgency among the young.

Levi A. Holmes II: Another problem was when we had large events like a dinner dance, we were only drawing 60 people for the event. The Bronze Shields is a huge organization. If we only got 60 or 80 people coming to an event that used to attract hundreds of people, that's a problem. I watched what was happening and I made a mental note about what was right and what was wrong with the organization.

Larry Brown: When it got time for me to retire, the basketball team had run its course. They were doing the same things. Different leadership started changing, especially when the younger officers came into the police department. They didn't buy into the Bronze Shields philosophy as far as the old ideals we had, like being a part of the community. Seemed like the whole psyche of these young guys was to become detectives. And the only way to do that was to get close to the politicians. That's where a big part of the breakdown happened within the Bronze Shields. As a result, they started losing a lot of support. Even the Bronze Shields dances weren't what they used to be because they became so political. At every dance, you were honoring somebody or had to honor somebody. And that person was a politician. So, the community started to get left out. It wasn't the same thing. The venue changed. Used to be Symphony Hall. Then it became the Terrace Ballroom and the different hotels. The whole concept and philosophy behind the dance changed which caused it to lose a lot of support. People who used to support the Bronze Shields dances stopped coming.

Ronald Glover: To me, the Bronze Shields had become mostly about parties. The organization was just a party. They weren't doing anything in a way I'd envisioned. No real activism or community service. Just parties. I wanted more community involvement to let people know the Bronze Shields are here, that Black police officers are here. We have a voice.

Carrie Reed: For a while, it was basically the same people and same members doing the same things year after year. There was no new blood coming out. We weren't putting the word out about what we were doing. We had meetings but they didn't push for members or new recruits to come out. But toward the end of the decade members like Anthony Kerr, Ronald Glover and Levi Holmes stepped up and helped the organization bloom again.

James Du Bose: A new and younger generation of Bronze Shields members gave a boost to the morale and productivity. Under the leadership of members like Anthony Kerr and Ronald Glover, the legacy and tradition of the Bronze Shields was re-established and moved forward.

Anthony Kerr: People already knew me from the beard issue. So I had some credibility. Even though that happened in 1998, people still remembered that I was a person who would stand up for an issue. I put values in front of social order. People found they could talk to me. And if I made a statement to the *Star-Ledger* newspaper people thought, "Wow, the Bronze Shields is taking a stance on an issue."

Carrie Reed: Everyone began doing something for the organization's rebirth. Each new president was able to accomplish something that opened up a door for the Bronze Shields that, in prior years had closed.

Anthony Kerr: You get to the year 2000, and the Bronze Shields looks like it's in free-fall. When I say free-fall, I mean going down fast. The bar we owned had been mismanaged. It was not being monitored. With a cash business like that, people tend to steal. No one was in charge. They would run the bar, but no one did reports on how much money was coming in or going out. Also, no one was paying any of the organization's bills. When I became president one of our members, Alonzo Evans, who had been a great Bronze Shields president, gave me the keys to the building and told me to increase the membership. I think we were down to 200 members or less. But there were 300 Black police officers in the department. The first thing I discovered was that the building was $21,000 in debt. It was also one step away from foreclosure. The utility bill was $7000. The tax bill was $14,000. This was left by the previous administrations. I think when the bar was left unchecked it just became a cash cow for whoever was managing it. There was absolutely no accountability. We also had membership dues. That was bringing in around $1000 a month. That's not going to pay for commercial insurance or taxes or the water bill. I also found out there was someone listed on the property as the agent of the building. That person was waiting until our headquarters went into foreclosure. Then he would just come and take the property. And mind you, I didn't work 9 to 5 for the police department. I worked around the clock and I'd just become a lieutenant or something. At the same time I had a bad Bronze Shields board of trustees around me when I became the president. Having a bad board works against you because, you need help to be successful. You can't be a one-man army. And when I took office, even board members weren't coming to the meetings. They were used to the organization being lethargic. No activities, no business sense, and no sense of progress. When we were supposed to meet, I'd open the bar on Sunday. And no one came. I complained to one of the former presidents, Robert Braswell, who was the son of Horace Braswell. I said I wasn't getting help and no one was coming to the meetings. Robert told me to just put the Bronze Shields under what's called "emergency operation." He said, "Once you do that you can make executive decisions." Immediately afterward, I sent notices to all the board members who were not showing up. I said, "If you miss a second meeting, I'm taking you off the board." Then I started putting my own people on the board. These were competent people. They had accounting degrees. They took over the financial books for the bar. My instructions were, "If you can't find the financial records for the bar, shut it down for now." We went in and took action. We began to rebuild this thing. We re-established order and accountability. Next, we started getting in the newspapers again. We started taking a stand on issues. We started making statements letting the politicians know how many people we were tied to in the community. If they hear you as a unified voice, then they start to listen to you. And because of these steps, we began to build our membership back. We started putting a newsletter out. We asked questions about officers' concerns. By the time I left office we were back in the 300-members range. That's because I kept banging the drum. We also started dealing with the finances. I'd shut the bar down for a moment. Now all we had were membership dues. So we just worked on paying our bills. After that we went from being $27,000 in debt to being $14,000 in the black. We had a surplus. That saved the building. We got the lawyer's name removed from the property, the person who was sitting there waiting to take the building. It was a tremendous undertaking getting the Bronze Shields back on its feet.

Derrick Hatcher, Bronze Shields, NPD (1987-2012): Sheilah was also the member who also set the organizing back in motion. We don't like to talk about this, but people began to lose interest in the Bronze Shields right before Sheilah became president. She tried to get the rebuilding of the organization in motion. She got the wheels moving again. In the time we went from Sheilah to Ronald Glover as president the number of women in the Bronze Shields began to increase.

Levi A. Holmes II: Ronald Glover also significantly resuscitated the Bronze Shields, because before then we were busy getting back on our feet. Before Glover, nothing was going on. Labeeb Abdullah was also a good president, but he was more about doing police work in the community on a volunteer basis. He did community patrols in some of the neighborhoods and downtown Newark.

Anthony Kerr: Ronald Glover became president after me. He was one of the people I brought on the board of trustees when I first became president. Since I was having trouble with the old, lethargic board not showing up I brought in different people who either had social consciousness or had a skill set. Glover was college-educated and he had social connections. I needed people around me to move my agenda forward. I remember a time when I had to take a leave of absence from the Bronze Shields's presidency. It was for a week or more. I submitted a letter to the membership putting Glover in as acting president. He later told me that moment helped him decide to run for president. As a result, he became the president after me.

Ronald Glover: Anthony Kerr, who was the president at the time, challenged me to join. Back then I had a lot of pent-up anger. There were a lot of things—in society, in life, and on the job—that I thought were unfair. There were also things Kerr challenged me to join as a way to direct my feelings. I didn't know much about the Bronze Shields at the time. And he put me on the board of trustees.

Anthony Kerr: Glover did what he felt he needed to do. He kept the social events going. He brought in his board of trustees. He also brought in his people. They moved forward, and afterward everything was passed on to the next person.

Ronald Glover: I started going to the meetings. I started voicing my opinion at meetings. I brought ideas to the meeting. I became more vocal and more involved. After a while Kerr would let me run the meetings.

Gene Etchison: Glover brought the new energy.

Niles Wilson: Under Glover's presidency I remember one of our challenges was to get back on the street and have our voices heard. The Bronze Shields needed to protest black-on-black violence. We, as an organization needed to say, "Hey, let's stop the killing."

Bryan Morris: Besides the Christmas and Thanksgiving events, we also continued what Labeeb had done and organized community patrols and block watch events. We'd get out and teach people about government and how it works for them.

Ronald Glover: The one thing I did when I became president was put the Bronze Shields back in the public. I made sure we had a stronger presence in events like Newark's Black Heritage Parade. I felt Black officers should be in the parade more than working the parade and providing security. I wanted the Bronze Shields to know that this parade was ours as a people. Another thing I did was initiate a program called Safe Passages with schools. We coordinated with the principals via walkie-talkies to make sure kids got to school and home safely. Around this time there were a lot of shootings going on in Newark. We also did Black history programs. We did book bag drives for kids. And, contrary to how some officers felt about the protests led by Ras Baraka against brutality, I attended many of the marches as a representative of the Bronze Shields. I enjoyed the fire Baraka brought back to the community.

Niles Wilson: Under Ron Glover's presidency we also tackled the senseless killings in Newark. But that could get tricky at times. He tried to work with Newark's street activists like Larry Hamm, the head of the People's Organization for Progress. Glover offered to march in solidarity with his organization against street violence. Hamm flat-out refused. He wanted nothing to do with police officers. Glover tried to get the Bronze Shields involved with other Newark-based movements, but we'd get rejected. We did eventually work with activists like Earl "Street Doctor" Best and his Street Warriors organization. We also worked with some clergy groups. Anyone who said yes, we worked with them.

James Du Bose: The Bronze Shields gave a motorcycle rally to raise money for computers at the William Brown Academy.

Gene Etchison: After Glover got the Bronze Shields back out into the community, Levi officially brought it all the way back. He took the organization over the wall.

Levi A. Holmes II: When I was in the academy, I asked people about the Bronze Shields. After joining, I knew someday I'd be president. I'd had leadership and activist experience in college. That experience gave me a great foundation. I always knew where my passion was. And I loved the city of Newark. All the time I spent in the Bronze Shields, going to the meetings, I would talk to whoever the president was and find out what they were doing. I'd also try and see how I could be involved. When I felt I was in a position to possibly run for president I recruited 13 people to ride with me in my bid for the slot. And when I ran, I did it like an actual campaign with those people campaigning for me to be president. We handed out flyers. We did a polling site. And I won unanimously.

Anthony Kerr: Everything I dreamed of doing with the Bronze Shields I didn't get a chance to accomplish. Levi had been able to make it happen. He changed the bylaws. You now have to participate in a certain amount of meetings if you want to run for president. You also have to have a business plan if you want to run for president. No more lack of accountability and oversight.

Levi A. Holmes II: My first order of business as president was to continue making sure the organization was financially stable. We were still unstable during this time. Our building was paid for. We were still getting dues from payroll deductions. There were no major bills. But I still had to correct all the financial business. I had to go to court with the IRS and represent the organization. In court I tried to reduce our debt. We had a great treasurer at the time. We organized our funds and started paying off whoever we owed money to. After six months we were debt-free. The next thing I did was change our bylaws. They weren't updated. And they weren't professionally written. The bylaws are the backbone of an organization. Some of the by-laws had to be removed because we're a non-profit organization, a 501c3. And as such, we can't discriminate. Yet, in the bylaws, it stated as a rule that one of your parents had to be African American. You have to be able to prove one of your parents was an African American to join. I knew that was a violation, and it would become an issue if the organization ever became relevant again. If that was exposed, we'd lose our status as a non-profit. So I got rid of it. There were other changes like the definitions of titles—but those were technical matters. We eliminated the freedom to loan money to members. After the by-laws were cleared up, we took care of the building. It was antiquated. We had fundraisers to help renovate the building. We also called for what was called "Unity Day." We called all the neighboring police departments around the county— East Orange, Irvington, Hillside and the prosecutors' office—and invited them to our headquarters to fellowship and bond. That let our members know that we were actively engaging other police departments. You need relationships to work in this world. Unfortunately, in cities we allow borders to separate us. I can't bond with you because you're a Newark police officer and I'm an Irvington officer. That's nonsense. That created more unity. It got our brand back out there and it raised money. It also got all Bronze Shields members involved—not just the executive board.

Sheilah Coley: One of the conversations I had with Levi when he thought about running for president was about the importance of having a supportive group around you. I told him he needed a core group. That's what I had. That's what I credited to my success as president. Once he had that, I told him to build upon the group. But the most important thing I told him was you can't do anything without the community. I said, "You need to get back out in the community and start rebuilding the Bronze Shields."

Levi Holmes II: I changed our mentoring program. As it stood, we only saw the kids once a month. You can't have an impact on a kid if you just see her or him once a month. So we created what we called the Police Explorers. Basically, it was a junior police academy. We'd engage the children two days a week, two hours a day, all year round. One day would be physical fitness, getting them into shape. The next day would be learning, a class where we'd teach them the laws and the courtroom. We teach classroom etiquette and public speaking. That gave us a constant relationship with them.

Carrie Reed: We did scholarships with the children. We did a walk to raise money to help fight cancer. We recruited for the NAACP. We did semi-political work helping to support candidates. That was something we weren't supposed to do as a group. But as individuals we could do what we wanted to. We were still involved in getting members promoted within the police department. We continued to advocate for more representation within the police department. This was under Sharpe James and later, Cory Booker. We attended political events in full force. We'd wear something to let them know we were Bronze Shields members. Whoever the president of the Bronze Shields was—at that time it was Ronald Glover—he would meet with the politician and make the case for a promotion. We held rallies and put out press releases to make our voices heard.

Levi A. Holmes II: We did the usual things: we did a book drive for the schools and students. We did those regularly. But I wanted to do tangible things. I wanted the organization to do something that had more impact. I figured in a city like Newark, where the population is mostly Black and the politicians are mostly Black and the police department has a higher percentage of African Americans than other cities, that the Bronze Shields should be able to speak to City Hall about what we wanted.

Carrie Reed: Glover had ideas and Levi had ideas. Glover was about empowering people and moving us forward. But they did it amongst a small click of people. We didn't have a wide range of activities. Levi was also moving us forward, but it was done in a way that was open and across a broad group of members. Many of us who were members under Glover were still members under Levi. So it was easy to see the difference. But between the two it was a matter of different ideas to achieve the same goals. A lot of presidents before them had direction but it was more geared toward themselves and progressing themselves as opposed to advancing the organization. Under Glover, we did things out in the community. Under Levi the activities—those ideas—had been expanded. And because of that, the Bronze Shields expanded. Each year it was a new project for us. We kept the old things and we added on new ones. We'd go to the churches and other organizations and events. We weren't doing that before. And as a result, we expanded our presence within the community. We were known amongst the people again.

Niles Wilson: Going into the 2000s, the organization was in pretty good shape. You got more participation and more events.

Levi A. Holmes II: The executive board I inherited as the president pushed back. They all quit the organization because they said I didn't know what I was doing. They said I was inexperienced at running an organization and that I would kill the Bronze Shields. Not only did they refuse to participate, but they didn't show up to any events to help.

John L. Smith: Younger officers with a different thought process came on the force. They thought they got on the force because of their looks and their smarts. That changed heading into the 21st Century with young guys like Glover and Levi, who knew the value of the organization. They re-established a sense of unity in the organization. The Bronze Shields always had mentorship among its members. The issue was were there any leaders who could add to that mentoring and organizational legacy.

Levi A. Holmes II: I was more community-oriented and Glover was more corporate-focused. He was more inclusive and in line with the police department's administration. He was about corporate relationships. He would focus on working with the police director who, at that time, was Garry McCarthy. Or he would have an event and the co-sponsor would be Prudential or the energy company PSE&G or the New Jersey Devils hockey team. I thought the Bronze Shields should focus on connecting more with the community. That's where we came from and that's where we needed to be.

Bryan Morris: Levi got the Bronze Shields back into the community again. It's that simple. He put a face back on the organization. The Bronze Shields was again seen as a community organization, fighting for the rights of the people and Black cops. Remember when the organization was founded, it was a benevolent association fighting for the rights of Black cops who were being disenfranchised and disrespected. Initially, they were the ones needing protection. The organization was born out of the idea that, hey, the union is not looking out for us. Let's look out for ourselves.

Newark was also going through another transition. After five terms as Newark's second African American mayor, Sharpe James helped usher in noticeable improvements to the city's business and cultural image, seeing the completion of the much-heralded New Jersey Performing Arts Center and, eventually, the Prudential Center sports arena. Even violent crimes in Newark dropped dramatically from 10,000 in the early '90s to under 5,000 per year by 1999. On the flip side, James's administration was also stained with charges of corruption. In 1997 Police Director William Celester, who James recruited from Boston, pleaded guilty to charges of fraud. James's chief of staff, Jackie Mattison, resigned after being found guilty of accepting bribes. And James's run for a sixth term was upended in 2006 when he was charged with (and later convicted of) fraud. After Sharpe refused to seek another four years Newark elected Cory Booker, a polished, suburban-raised community advocate. Running on a reformist platform, Booker vowed to improve Newark's education/city services, greatly reduce crime and rid City Hall of corruption. His knack for cultivating national publicity and social media attention brought a renewed interest in Newark, which was now seen as a city boldly struggling to make its way toward progress and a renaissance. But, amongst the Bronze Shields, the new mayor's agenda didn't feel like it included their ideas or input about the future.

Levi A. Holmes II: Once Sharpe became so powerful it was like he became the emperor. That's how powerful he was. Whatever he said was law. And people began to resent that. If you went up against him in a situation, you had no support. Once he said no, it's no. No follow-up conversation. No alternate court to decide your argument. It's over. And all the people who resented Sharpe having that kind of power jumped on the Cory Booker bandwagon when Sharpe was convicted.

Ronald Glover: As the Bronze Shields was getting reestablished, Newark was also heading for a change. In 2006, when I became Bronze Shields president, I had to handle the rifts that arose within the group over what mayoral candidate we should support. At that time, the argument was whether we should support Sharpe James or Cory Booker.

Anthony Kerr: Cory didn't succeed in his first run for mayor. But he won on his second attempt. I think a part of that win was because, economically, Newark appeared to be okay. As a result, people felt comfortable with changing leadership. But that comfort was because of the stability Sharpe James created. And all he did was what mayors do: they get money for the city from various sources. He was also a senator, so he had access to money for the city coming from the state. But after a while the federal government stopped sending money to the state and the state stopped sending money to Newark.

Tijuana Burton: Newark residents loved Sharpe James. Senior citizens loved him. Kids loved him. There were always programs, summer youth jobs, and other things for the community. During his tenure, a lot of the Boys and Girls Clubs were thriving. He took care of the police department. We had the equipment we needed. He supported us with promotions. This doesn't excuse what he was found guilty of. Finding that out was painful for everyone. Everyone was hurt when he was convicted. It was painful to know he'd done something so wrong when he'd been doing so many things right. So it was like, "Really. He was doing that."

Levi A. Holmes II: I didn't know Sharpe personally. But I watched him as the mayor. I loved what he did for the police department and the city. He hired police officers in record numbers, 100 or 150 graduating at a time from the police academy. It was great. I loved the fact he could speak to anyone. He could go to the Hilton Hotel in the suburbs and have everyone love him. That same day, he can go to the projects, speak and everyone loved him. He could touch people. Because of that, I had great respect for him. He also had a different ideal when it came to fighting crime. As far as the Bronze Shields went, he still supported us. He came to our events when he could. Toward the end, we weren't a priority to him. But we also showed him he wasn't a priority to us. But he still loved us. To this day, he wears his Bronze Shields varsity jacket. He walks around Newark with that jacket on proud as ever.

Anthony Kerr: Cory won the election after Sharpe was convicted. That helped Cory out because Sharpe decided not to run for another term. More of the officers supported Cory when he ran the second time. His campaign message was, "Yes, I hear you. We're going to try and do something different." We thought if Cory won, the Bronze Shields would have a direct say in who would become the next police director, which is typical. We have another Black mayor who usually gives us that favor.

Levi A. Holmes II: Once Sharpe got stigmatized as being a criminal that swayed everyone. It slowed down public support and support from the police. When Sharpe was convicted it pushed more police to support Booker.

Anthony Kerr: Sharpe was on the fence about running again. And Cory was beating the drum about being mayor during Sharpe's last term. He'd also become more of a political force. Now there was a tidal wave of voters who wanted to join Cory's team. With that kind of support, he slipped right into office. He won by overwhelming numbers for two terms.

Levi A. Holmes II: When I was sworn in as Bronze Shields president Cory Booker spoke at the ceremony. Other than that we had no relationship. Once Cory won the election, he didn't support the Bronze Shields. He didn't come to any of our events. Nothing. He didn't get too involved with the police department either. Booker had a horrible relationship with the Bronze Shields. I found out later it was because some of us also supported Clifford Minor's run for mayor. Minor was a Bronze Shields member who ran against him. As a result, Cory felt he didn't have to deal with us. He didn't need us.

Mae Smith: I was a detective for 17 years. When Cory Booker became the mayor, I was bumped back down to patrol officer. That had everything to do with politics. Booker became the new mayor, and at the time I was a part of what they called the Executive Dignitary Protections. I was a part of Sharpe James's security team. After Booker took office, all of the officers from my squad got moved back to patrol. That was his way of showing he had strength. He wanted to punish everybody.

Levi A. Holmes II: It's not a matter of need. It's a matter of respect. He said he didn't need to meet with us. We'd invite him to our events: unity day, dinner dance, whatever. Cory Booker wouldn't come. Not only would he not come, but he also wouldn't respond to our invitation. One time, I sent a nasty email to him saying show us the courtesy you would show anyone in the street. You can at least thank us for the invitation and then say you can't make it. After I did that, he started showing up to events. But we had limited interactions with him.

Ronald Glover: I remember when we celebrated the 50th anniversary of the Bronze Shields. I invited him to speak. He showed up for that event.

Mae Smith: The Bronze Shields had a relationship with Cory Booker that was almost non-existent. Did he ever have a close relationship with any of our members? No. Some of us who supported him, as they had a right to do.

Janet Bostic: Cory Booker definitely brought gentrification. But the reality is Mayor Gibson did the initial groundwork and Sharpe James did unbelievably great things bringing business interest back to Newark with the New Jersey Performing Arts Center (NJPAC). I didn't think white people would come into Newark to go see performances. But they did and they do.

Levi A. Holmes II: The city was changing under Cory Booker. The complexion of the city was changing. The face of City Hall was changing. Booker brought in people who were not from Newark, which rubbed a lot of people the wrong way. Under Cory there were plenty of outsiders coming in. Cory was also a huge supporter of charter schools. That put him in a bad light with residents. Newark, at the time, was trying to get control back of its school system from the state. Cory was also supportive of people who had money. If you had money and wanted something in this city, you got it.

In his attempt at a fresh approach to fighting crime, Mayor Cory Booker bypassed the Newark Police Department and recruited the city's new police director from New York City. Former NYPD commander Garry McCarthy, who is Irish, was credited with drastically reducing violent crime in a drug-ridden Manhattan neighborhood via unwarranted stops and massive arrests. The story of how Booker brought McCarthy and his same zero-tolerance policy of fighting crime to Newark began a new chapter in the Newark Police Department.

Anthony Kerr: This was also during a time when we were arguing that we wanted changes within the police department. But the word was that Cory was getting his directive from Mike Bloomberg, the mayor of New York City. Was it true? Who knows? But he did hire a police director from NYC.

Sheilah Coley: A lot of people were not happy about Garry McCarthy being brought in. We thought we had enough qualified people within our police department to move up and do the job. But at the time, Booker's thinking was, "If I bring someone from outside of Newark then that person would be more objective."

Anthony Kerr: Cory Booker started turning folks off. He especially started turning off Black police officers when he hired McCarthy.

Ronald Glover: I felt like Cory Booker snubbed Black officers with his decision. I held a press conference to voice my opinion. Afterward, I got called into several meetings regarding that and other issues.

Anthony Kerr: McCarthy had a middle management team that was close to him. They influence on his decisions. It was a matter of if someone had McCarthy's ear and he asked, "How is this Bronze Shields organization?" The person might say, "Well, it's just a few of them. They aren't that strong." McCarthy might say, "Well, the mayor thinks they're strong." The person would tell McCarthy we weren't all that. This would deflate our power to the police director. Afterward, the Bronze Shields didn't get a lot of cooperation out of McCarthy.

Carrie Reed: I didn't like that decision. But I guess when Cory became mayor, he'd made some deals. That's what politicians have to do and sometimes the deals are underhanded. You make a promise, and you have to follow it through.

Anthony Kerr: Sharpe James was a great mayor because he promoted people from within the city. He rarely brought in people from outside. If someone had to vacate a position, someone from Newark took that person's space. That was a good thing because that meant many of the jobs went to Black people.

Gene Etchison: We thought we'd get Robert Rankin as the police director. A lot of people felt betrayed by Cory, especially the Black and Latino community. When Cory Booker ran, he made promises that he would hire from within the department—but he didn't.

Anthony Kerr: Cory Booker didn't consult with us on our next selection, and we'd picked a candidate with deep integrity. It was Robert Rankin. But lo and behold, Cory brought in McCarthy. There wasn't much we could do. We'd made our suggestion. But Cory had come in with this showman mentality like he was going to save the day?

Tijuana Burton: When McCarthy was brought in, the Booker administration thought he'd be the savior.

Anthony Kerr: McCarthy came in knowing that the current structure of the Newark Police Department could potentially be hurtful to Black people. He eventually came to a Bronze Shields meeting and we discussed this. Ronald Glover was the president of the organization at that time. McCarthy gave us a speech about there being no more us-against-them and no more haves-and-have-nots. Then he said to the police department that he was here to make a change.

Bryan Morris: McCarthy, who's a New Yorker, had this gunslinger mentality.

Mae Smith: I had friends who were NYC police officers. They told me and some others that if we had any influence with Mayor Booker, tell him to not hire McCarthy.

Gene Etchison: Ronald Glover had leverage with McCarthy because Glover's sister was on the national board of the NAACP, and McCarthy didn't want that kind of fight. So Ronald could get a meeting with McCarthy. No one messed with Ronald because his sister could get a rally around him.

Bryan Morris: I think Glover was the start of us getting back some cooperation with the police department. Or I should say he started to get that reconnection for us.

Levi A. Holmes II: There was a time when McCarthy was giving African American officers hell. But we were with Ras Baraka, who'd become the South Ward councilman. One time, McCarthy mistreated our supervisor—a captain—and we asked to meet with him. He wouldn't even give us the courtesy of a meeting. So we called Ras and told him McCarthy wouldn't meet with us. Ras brought the thunder to him, called him up and let him have it. He spoke on our behalf and told McCarthy that it's unacceptable to disrespect the Bronze Shields. After that McCarthy called us into a meeting and he was on fire. He let us know how upset he was. Since I was the Bronze Shields president, I stated that McCarthy was wrong for putting this Black captain on patrol in the cellblock when he should be out here being a leader for other officers. Give him a precinct or something. After some back and forth, McCarthy put the captain back in a precinct. He was put in charge of the 4th Precinct. I made my case. At the end of the meeting we got what we wanted.

Tijuana Burton: When Cory brought McCarthy in, we developed a zero-tolerance policy when it came to policing.

Claude Coleman: To be honest, that kind of policing started under Sharpe. When I became police director, the first thing he wanted me to do was to go out and make arrests—lock people up. That's why when I hear people talk about Joe Biden and Hillary Clinton and the crime policies that were enacted in the '90s, I remember how it locked so many people up. You have to remind people of that, in the early '90s, mayors like Sharpe and Harold Washington in Chicago and the mayor from Baltimore, and other Black mayors were begging someone to do something more about crime. We, as a community, were begging law enforcement to put people in jail.

Derrick Hatcher: McCarthy stepped up aggressive patrolling in certain neighborhoods. And officers stepped up and followed those orders exactly. The gang situation overall became horrible. The gangs were multiplying in numbers. They were killing each other and people in the community. We had to take action. The cops went out and did what we were supposed to do.

Sheilah Coley: Cory Booker did about as best he could with the resources he had. That was during a time when Newark really found itself struggling to keep the lights on. Cory Booker's administration was when we had to, again, lay-off police officers.

Niles Wilson: We had a serious gang situation in Newark that started in the early '90s. Then it just kept growing because the gangs in Newark were basically about nothing but drug dealing. It just became a coordinated group of people who identified with a particular gang. Bloods and Crips in Newark were different than the ones in California. It's a different mindset geared toward drug sales. Over the years those gangs had gotten more violent, especially the younger members.

Tijuana Burton: One of the things Cory Booker did was have the bodegas and chicken spots close at 10 o'clock, like stores close in the suburbs. Before that, those places would stay open until 2 or 3 in the morning—like a bar. They were also a safe haven for crime. People would go there and get knocked in the head and robbed. Then here we come to solve the crime. So Cory had these places close early to see if it would cut down on unnecessary crime. His thinking was that if it worked in the suburbs it might work in Newark. I don't think it lasted long because city people need to go to the store at midnight and 1 am. I don't think that the new rule went very well.

Sheilah Coley: There were different interpretations of zero-tolerance. People thought with that, cops would just snatch people off the street for any reason and lock them up. That's not what we were doing. We were focused on high-crime areas. If we believed there was no reason for you to be standing on the corner, then we'd ask you to move on. And in essence, that's what we were doing.

Tijuana Burton: But it got to the point where you couldn't stand on the street corner. And if you were on the corner, we're going to find out why. But you also understand that people have a right to be on the corner. If I'm not committing a crime, then leave me alone. But we adopted a zero-tolerance approach to everything.

Sheilah Burton: We also started enforcing quality-of-life laws, which turned things around for us. We would address drinking in public instead of riding by to get to real crime. We addressed lewdness even though you say you couldn't find a bathroom and decided to make the side of this building your bathroom. We started enforcing juvenile curfew to stop kids from hanging out at all times of the night and becoming victims of crimes.

Niles Wilson: To fight crime, we focused on mapping. We used computer mapping and every crime was mapped. When a certain incident happened a colored dot was placed on the map. All the crime was color-coded. There was one color for murder, another color for robbery and one for stolen autos. And wherever the dots were that's where we'd put law enforcement. If you had a lot of drug sales on a particular street during certain hours, then the commander was responsible for coordinating with the precinct and the narcotics squad to make sure we hit that area. What did the commanders want? They wanted to see a lot of police interaction in the neighborhood. They wanted field interrogations, which is stopping someone and checking to make sure they don't have a warrant. So basically, the precinct commanders were responsible for tackling a particular crime that plagued their area. On top of that, they had to report all that they'd done in handling the crimes or preventing the crimes. And as a result, you saw 20 burglaries in a particular area drop down to two. So that was effective. If what a commander accomplished didn't work, he or she would be asked what new strategy was going to be used in order to be effective. The commanders were expected to show the director they had a plan of action. Then, you had to show results.

Tijuana Burton: McCarthy was new, but he wasn't that innovative. He thought Newark's crime rate was a piece of cake to manage. He eventually saw it wasn't. He learned that he needed to be more open to what people were saying. He came in from the big city with his ego on his shoulder. Cory's administration thought McCarthy was so smart in terms of fighting crime. But he wasn't community-oriented. And when he had to deal with the community, most of the time he sent a representative.

Sheilah Coley: The policy didn't backfire so much as different officer's interpretation of the policy did. Different officers understood zero-tolerance differently. Then again that phrase is a blanket statement. For me, it meant that if I have an area or neighborhood I'm responsible for, I should know everyone who is functioning normally in my area. If I know that then I know who doesn't belong there and who does. I'm not trying to violate anyone's civil rights. But I have to ask a person, "Are you here to visit someone?" That opens a conversation. If they don't know anyone there and are just hanging out, you can inform them it's not a place to hang and that these residence don't want people hanging in front of their homes.

Tijuana Burton: There's a way to police and get compliance. But, at some point, it was us demanding people get off the street. And we'd get them off the street by any means. And you can't do that. You can't bark at people. Not everyone is going to comply. The problem became how we were trying to get people to comply. Now, don't get me wrong, in some areas of Newark that approach was warranted.

Carrie Reed: I also noticed a very troubling trend that was going on in Newark, some of which I've witnessed. A lot of officers were locking up a lot of Black children and giving them every charge that they could give them so the kids couldn't have a chance of going to college or become officers or anything that could be messed up by having a criminal record.

Tijuana Burton: After a while the people began to resist. They began to challenge us on how we policed them, which created a growing tension between the police and the community. As someone who worked in Internal Affairs, I noticed civilian complaints against the Newark police were increasing.

Levi A. Holmes II: More complaints happened under Cory Booker and Garry McCarthy because they were not really engaged with the community. Cory Booker wasn't a community guy at all. Neither was McCarthy. That especially doesn't look right when complaints are coming in about the police. And crime is going through the roof, shootings, and murders. That's trouble when the two main people in charge are not engaging the residents.

Bryan Morris: When you go into the police academy, there's already this mentality they drill into you. It's us-versus-them. There are the police, the blue line that is the "us" and then there are those people we police. That's the "them." They are the enemy. In a place like Newark, which is over 50 percent Black, who's getting the brunt of this mentality? After being in the Bronze Shields you get a level of social consciousness about who you're policing and how you must interact with them. You realize we're not here to knock heads. We're here to save heads. When we see police brutality, we don't engage in it—we stop it.

Labeeb Abdullah: People like Braswell and Bostic were a breath of fresh air to the community. Then somehow later on—I don't know how—we as police, became an air of disgust. Some of us just didn't do the right thing.

Gene Etchison: The Newark Police Department had to be

watched because it was getting brutal at the time. A lot of us were making unnecessary stops. We were violating people's civil rights. You did have cops doing that, and people knew which ones were doing it. Some didn't look like us and some did. As an officer you can use discretion. But it had gotten so bad with stops and arrests that some people who were slated to become officers got caught in those stops, got arrested for bullshit, and could no longer apply for a job with the police department.

Chapter 7

BRONZE AND BEYOND

Not long after the Bronze Shields celebrated its 50th anniversary the Newark Police Department received an unflattering national spotlight when the American Civil Liberties Union (ACLU) petitioned the Department of Justice to investigate civil rights violations and false arrests committed by officers. The three-year probe, while unearthing a number of abuses and misconduct, resulted in much-needed changes, signaling a new era for the Newark Police Department and the Bronze Shields.

Tijuana Burton: I thought the investigation was needed because things were becoming a bit much. We were starting to get a lot of complaints from the community on how we were policing. By that point we needed someone to oversee this. We needed a fresh pair of eyes to examine the complaints and let us know we weren't going about things in the right way. It wasn't too bad, but we needed to be told we could do better.

Sheilah Coley: Before the ACLU came in, Internal Affairs handled those types of investigations and presented the reports or complaints. We'd say we have this many complaints. Some complaints were internal and others were external. We'd say we have one or two repeat officers. That was all the info we would have. It was simple. Once McCarthy came in, Internal Affairs was no longer a part of the complaint investigation process.

Levi A. Holmes II: No one likes to tell the truth about the Newark Police Department because you have to display your ugly side. The truth was the ACLU was needed to an extent. But it was not as bad as the ACLU made it out to be. It was simply a matter of the department's report systems. When we made a stop or encountered an incident or interacted with the community, there was a form we filled out. We'd make a report. On the form it never required us to fill out a justification for the stop. All the form asked for was what you did and when you did it. We weren't asked to justify our stops. It didn't ask officers why they made stops. So when the investigation happened, the ACLU saw our files. They saw that a lot of reports had no explanations of why people were stopped. They just saw people were stopped. Doing reports that way help pad the police department's stats. It made it look like we were actually doing our job. But the other side of that was we actually were doing a lot of unjustified stops. We did them because we're the police and folks had to get off the corner.

Sheilah Coley: It didn't create confusion as much as we officers just didn't know what our department was in charge of. We also didn't know what was going on. The only information we knew about was what went on in our individual commands. We also knew which officers we were getting the most complaints about.

Derrick Hatcher: It was sad that the ACLU said we weren't trained properly and not following police procedures. I disagreed with that indictment of the department.

Sheilah Coley: There wasn't enough oversight In the Internal Affairs' investigative process. One thing the ACLU said was, "How can you have this many investigations and all are unfounded, and you only sustained one? How is that possible?" When the ACLU investigation began, I was assigned to Internal Affairs to bring that department up to standard. The first thing I did was ask for an audit by the Essex County Prosecutors Office. They came in and did an audit. They audited the number of investigations of police misconduct done by the Newark Police Department. They looked at the quality of the investigations and their outcomes. I was assigned to clean up the process of recording these investigations. That's why I called for an audit. The result was I was able to see that some of the investigators lost their objectivity and their reports were based more on friendships within the police department than facts. I shared my findings with then-police director Samuel DeMaio. He transferred some of those officers who were guilty of playing with the facts. Then we put different standards and policies in place.

Tijuana Burton: They went around to each department to interview officers and supervisors. They came to Internal Affairs. They took a boatload of paperwork. They reviewed many of the investigations. They wanted to see the type of complaints we were getting and how the complaints were handled. They looked at what the outcomes of the complaints were. They looked at whether we were properly communicating with the public and being transparent. They were there for a few years investigating. After they presented their findings, there was a consent decree that exposed what was seen as the problem. And they set guidelines on how the Newark Police Department will handle matters from now on.

Anthony Kerr: That investigation and bringing in civil rights violations led to much-needed reforms. The civilian complaints, which were championed by the ACLU, helped make changes.

Tijuana Burton: By the time I retired they began to implement the consent decree.

Sheilah Coley: We'd also met with the ACLU and asked them what their complaints were. We'd tell them what we could change, and legally what we couldn't address. As a result, we made some significant changes toward the end of the Booker administration.

While the ACLU/DOJ investigation signaled a fresh start for Newark's law enforcement policies it also coincided with a historic administrative change within the city as well as a major breakthrough for the Bronze Shields. In 2011, the organization's former president Sheilah Coley was promoted to Newark's chief of police. As the first woman to ever hold the position in the police department's 154-year history, Coley had broken a once immovable ceiling for women police officers. She came to symbolize the Bronze Shields's renewed fight for justice and power in the 21st Century.

Levi A. Holmes II: That was a homerun because the Bronze Shields got her that position. When I became president, we found out that the chief of police position might be available. We immediately went to the community to do the right thing. The Bronze Shields started interviewing people who might be candidates for the job. Sheilah was one of them. After the interviews, we selected her as our candidate. We went to the city council members because they're the ones who approve the position. We told them we wanted Sheilah Coley and gave them the reasons why. We held meetings with every councilperson.

Sheilah Coley: Levi, Anthony Roberts, and Walter Melvin came to my office a couple of times. They told me the police chief position was being reinstated because at one point it had been abolished. I was told they were looking for an African American to be the police chief. They asked if I was interested and I said, "Sure." That was the first conversation. Afterward, we had a few more subsequent meetings. Then they told me I'd make the best candidate. They asked if I was sure I wanted the position and again, I said yes.

Anthony Kerr: How could anyone fight against that appointment? She was a class-act administrator.

Sheilah Coley: In Newark, the mayor appoints the chief of police. The city council confirms the police director. Samuel DeMaio and I were going in as a package deal. He'd be approved as director and I would become police chief. Cory Booker brought a letter to the council while they were in session. He read the letter reinstating the chief of police position and that his nominee was me. The people in the audience started clapping. The council voted unanimously to reinstate the position. And as a symbolic gesture, they even gave their own vote for me, even though they didn't have to. We were in DeMaio's office watching this all play out on TV.

Tijuana Burton: That was a huge moment because she came out of my academy class. So she represented very well. During that time the department had a lag in female supervisors. Barbara George had passed away. Me and other women were moving up the rank. But Sheilah was moving a little faster than the rest of us. When she made it to chief status that was huge because it'd been so long since we'd seen a promotion of that caliber. And for her to go beyond the ranks to become the chief of police was amazing. It was the police director who controlled policy within the police department. But the police chief ran the entire department. Newark had never seen a woman chief of police before—let alone a Black one. That was a major accomplishment because it put women on the map again. People were proud.

Shakoor Mustafa: She knew the hurdles. But she had the wear-with-all to withstand any opposition. If you see a woman in a high-ranking position, you know she is more qualified than her male counterpart because she had to work 10 times as hard. It's the same thing that Black people have to go through. And whatever promotion Sheilah got she earned it.

Tijuana Burton: There were naysayers. But they didn't add up to much. In terms of leadership, there wasn't much negativity anyone could say about Sheilah. As a leader, she could be very stern. But as a woman, she couldn't be anything other than that. If you're a woman and you're perceived as soft or a pushover they use it as an example to show women aren't suited for police work. I've heard men talk about her being stern, but she needed to be that way. As a woman she couldn't have made it any other way.

Sheilah Coley: That first night I was overwhelmed. From that moment my life completely changed. It was like I never had a moment to myself. I couldn't go to the same places I used to because people would recognize me and the whole dynamic would change. Although I was happy about the position, and I did the best job I could, I began to feel like I was living in a fishbowl. I started spending a lot more time at home, enjoying my personal space. If I went out somewhere, I was now prepared for the expectation of being recognized and someone saying to me, "Aren't you...?" It'd gotten so bad that one day I'd gotten really sick and needed to be taken to the emergency room. They were hooking me up to IVs and I noticed that a lot of nurses kept coming in and out of the room. I thought they were just doing their job. Then finally, one of them said, "I saw you on TV with Cory Booker." Mind you, I'm in pain. But that's how bad the celebrity became for me.

Niles Wilson: When Cory Booker was mayor, he put a new spotlight on Newark. Sheilah becoming the first female police captain under his mayorship put Newark in the history books. He definitely knew this. But Cory Booker was politically ambitious. If something met his political aspirations, he was for it. If it didn't meet his aspirations, he didn't do it. Unfortunately, unlike Sharpe James, Cory Booker had no intentions of being mayor for three terms. He already had higher goals.

Sheilah Coley: Cory Booker became a senator shortly before the end of his second term. In his place, Councilman Luis Quintana became the interim mayor until the upcoming election.

Carrie Reed: By then the Bronze Shields leadership had developed a great relationship with Councilman Ras Baraka, who was running for mayor. He and Levi had a great rapport for a long time.

Levi A. Holmes II: When Ras Baraka ran for mayor after Cory moved to the senate, he got a lot of flack because he was accused of being a member of the Zoo Crew. This was mainly because he led protests organized by them after the Strawberry Daniels shooting. Was the Zoo Crew a gang or not? I wasn't sure. From what I know, it was a group of guys who hung together. They stuck together. And they had a vision of keeping their community active and safe. They started the Zoo Crew basketball league and all these community-based activities to help the community. They started a clothing merchandise business. They had retail stores. And what they did in the neighborhood actually worked. They were active. But in the police world, it was said they were criminals. And Ras Baraka was associated with them. Now even if it wasn't true, all you need are a group of police officers saying you're a criminal or associated with criminals. That gets everybody scrutinizing you. I didn't go for that. I knew Ras. I knew of his father. I knew Ras as a long-time activist who was about fighting for the people of Newark. Ras was smart and could articulate the problems and needs of Newark residence better than any of his opponents. But during the election, he couldn't overcome this conversation everyone was having about him being a criminal. As police, our collective bargaining union was the F.O.P. Because of our 501c3 status the Bronze Shields couldn't put our name out there as endorsing a candidate for an elected position. But we could endorse someone as an individual. The F.O.P. can endorse candidates. When it came time for them to meet and pick a candidate, the Bronze Shields flooded the meeting with our members. It was packed, standing room only. We even got some Latino and Portuguese officers to join us. In the meeting everyone was against Ras, saying he was a criminal. But we argued against them. We twisted the F.O.P.'s arm and got them to endorse Baraka for mayor. That was huge because getting police support was the only hurdle he had to overcome. Once he got that, all the rumors and chatter about him went away. Once the police endorsed him, that killed his competition. But there was also a police group of supervisors who were meeting about who they were going to endorse. I couldn't attend that meeting because I wasn't a supervisor. However, we called all the Black supervisors we knew and told them to endorse Ras for mayor. That meeting, I heard, was unbelievably hostile and heated. It was ugly. But we got enough people in the meeting to side with us. When it came time to vote it was split evenly—a stand-off. As a result, that group decided to stay out of it and endorse no one, which was cool. The F.O.P. endorsement was enough. Ras won in 2014. Right before Ras took office the Bronze Shields scored another landmark.

In another historic move Sheilah Coley was sworn in as Newark's police director in 2014.

Levi A. Holmes II: When DeMaio stepped down as director it was a natural progression for Sheilah to become police director. There was talk that there was going to be a nationwide search for a director, so we put in a word for Sheilah to make sure they considered her. We talked to the council people. We talked to Ras, who was still a councilman, and anyone who'd listen.

Sheilah Coley: Police Director Samuel DeMaio and I held our respective positions. Then in 2013 DeMaio decided to retire. Newark was also in between elections. The deputy mayor Luis Quintana and I had a great working relationship prior to me becoming chief and after I became police chief. He said he wanted to make me police director. I had to weigh the options because you're more protected as police chief. You're behind the scenes. But I thought, "Hey, in the worst-case scenario I can retire soon." So I said I'd be honored to accept the position.

Levi A. Holmes II: When Sheilah became director we threw her the biggest celebration ever. We had folks come from all over the state of New Jersey. And we held her tight. Whenever she had an engagement at a church or go to a community meeting, she had at least 10 Bronze Shields members guarding her. We elevated her. We bragged on her. We put the spotlight on her.

Sheilah Coley: Becoming the police director was historical. But by then, the media and the public had already become familiar with me. I did some interviews and got some press for becoming the director. But not nearly as much as I'd gotten when I became the police chief.

Tijuana Burton: Newark needed to see that. Not just the police department. The community needed to see that because she was community-oriented.

Gene Etchison: We lighted her achievement because she was one of ours. If anyone had anything negative to say about her promotion, they didn't say it because of fear. We were proud of her because she moved up the ranks.

Sheilah Coley: Shortly afterward I put my retirement papers in. I left because of that. But there was also some politics involved in my leaving. Every new administration comes in and they want to bring in their own people. And I knew that was a possibility. It had nothing to do with the quality of my work. It was a matter of Quintana stepping down as interim mayor and Ras Baraka coming in as the new mayor. He wanted to install his own chief and director.

Levi A. Holmes II: That was another homerun for the Bronze Shields, for real. We'd broken barriers over the last 60 years. But that truly showed how far we'd come.

The Bronze Shields celebrated 60 years of service in 2019. And with the coming of another anniversary members were moved to reflect...

Larry Brown: The Bronze Shields did a lot to change the culture within the Newark Police Department. There was a lot of racism in the police department. There was no upward mobility for people of color. If it weren't for the Bronze Shields there's no telling how long it would have taken for change to happen. I've seen police departments today that are still antiquated and racist. When I see stuff like that, I feel very proud of what the Bronze Shield accomplished.

Anthony Kerr: I wish some of the older members who've passed on could see the growth and progress the Bronze Shields have made. People like Alonzo Evans, who would be very, very happy, or James Du Bose who died a few years ago. He would be extraordinarily proud because he was a member in the 1950s when the organization started.

Niles Wilson: The legacy of the Bronze Shields is that it made it possible for African American, Latino and women officers to not only be employed by the department but to advance within the department. They could move into Internal Affairs, homicide investigation as well as be promoted through the ranks. The organization paved a way for that to happen. And even though there is a separate Latino police organization, the original charter of the Bronze Shields included Latino officers. We fought for them. Now, where will the Bronze Shields go in the future? That all depends on the leadership. It has to be someone who respects the past and has an eye for the future.

Sheilah Coley: It takes a lot to withstand the test of time the way the Bronze Shields has.

Louis Greenleaf: The Bronze Shields gave Black police officers a voice after all the years of not having one. And as a result, we've had several Black police directors. But all they have to do is stay in the community. Keep getting back to the community.

Ronald Glover: The work is in the trenches. And you've got to get out there and work with the people. Any time you take that uniform off or put it on, you're still a Black man or a Black woman. You can yell you're a cop as loud as you want, but you're still going to face society's perception of you. So there's a lot of work that still needs to be done.

Niles Wilson: A lot has changed in Newark since we started. There's a big debate in Newark about gentrification. The city decided to start building up certain areas. You started seeing companies like Whole Foods and Nike that you'd never see here. So when old stuff came down and new stuff started going up it was clear Newark was on the move. This affected the Bronze Shields because we sold our building. But what we've always done was make sure we didn't get wiped out in the process.

Gene Etchison: Floyd Bostic was like the godfather. Long after he retired, he stayed in touch with the Bronze Shields up until his death. It's guys like that who you never forget.

Janet Bostic: I am in awe at how brilliant my father was and what a great organizer he was. Toward the end of his life, he talked about the Bronze Shields a lot. He said it was something important that should go down in history and be documented.

Percell Goodwyn: I look at the police department now, and I see things are a lot easier for younger people. They still have to work hard, but the doors for advancement are open. I would credit that change to our work. Absolutely.

Bryan Morris: It was from being in the field and helping people, that members started to see that the people who we police also needed help too. Then we broadened our mission. It wasn't just about the cops, but also the people we serve. And if the community is behind you, that's always a big help. They scream louder than the cops do.

ACKNOWLEDGMENTS

First and foremost, thanks to Floyd Bostic Jr. for his vision and fortitude in helping establish the Bronze Shields, Inc., and for hosting the organization's inaugural meeting at his home on South 17th Street. Thanks to the founding members of the Bronze Shields for taking a stance for the future of Newark's Black police officers. Much thanks to Anthony Kerr and Ronald Glover for encouraging James Du Bose to coordinate and write the first incarnations of the Bronze Shields's history. That manuscript served as a huge part of this book's foundation. Also, thanks to Alexandra Jade Evans, Floyd Bostic Jr.'s granddaughter, who worked on a short documentary, along with Floyd, on the organization's early days. Footage from this project made it possible to include stories from the Bronze Shields's co-founders as well as the late Kenneth A. Gibson, Newark's first African American mayor. Thanks to the men and women of the Bronze Shields who've kept the mission alive for over 60 years. Thanks to Leonard McGhee and Calvin Larkins for helping to give the Bronze Shields a home at 43 William Street. Thanks to Levi A. Holmes II for bringing all the components together to help craft this book and see it through to completion. A special thanks to Ronke Idowu Reeves for proofreading and editing the book manuscript. And a huge thanks to Kyle Reeves for designing the book jacket. Lastly, this oral history couldn't have been told without the diligent cooperation of the Bronze Shields's past presidents, members, and associates who freely shared their memories and opinions about an untold part of Newark, NJ's dynamic and trailblazing past.

ABOUT THE AUTHORS

Marcus Reeves teaches journalism and hip-hop music history at New York University. He is the author of *Somebody Scream: Rap Music's Rise to Prominence in the Aftershock of Black Power*. His writing has appeared in *Playboy*, *The Crisis*, *Utne Reader*, *New York Times*, *San Francisco Chronicle*, and *The Washington Post*. He was born and raised in Newark, NJ.

James Du Bose had a career in law enforcement that spanned 50 years. After joining the NPD in 1956 he became one of the early members of the Bronze Shields. He also became the organization's historian. In 1963, Du Bose was recognized for helping save five children from a burning building in Newark. For his selfless service as a police officer and, later, director of security for the New Community Corporation, Du Bose was awarded the Medal of Honor by the Newark Police Department. He also wrote a Black history column for the *Clarion* newspaper. James Du Bose, a Newark native, died on October 29, 2015 at the age of 86.

BRONZE SHIELDS GRIOTS

Floyd Bostic Jr.

James Du Bose

Thomas Murray

Horace Braswell

Janet Bostic

Percell Goodwyn

James Nance

Charles Harris

Louis Greenleaf

John L. Smith

Derrick Hatcher

Niles Wilson

Leonard McGhee

Calvin Larkins

Sheilah Coley

Larry Brown

Junius Williams

Labeeb Abdullah

Charles Upshaw

Mae Smith

John Scott-Bey

Bryan Morris

Lance Owens

Mustafa Shakoor

Tijuana Burton

Carrie Reed

Donald Deans

Charles Knox

Kenneth Gibson

Harold Gibson

Levi A. Holmes II

Joseph Foushee

Anthony Kerr

Ronald Glover

Gene Etchison

Index

Abdul-Aziz, Farooq, 122, 125, 126

Abdullah, Labeeb, 105, 119, 152, 153

Addonizio, Hugh J., 11 – 14, 23 – 26, 38, 42 – 49, 74, 94

American Civil Liberties Union (ACLU), 172 – 175

Askin, Frank, 54

bank robberies, 73, 78 – 80

Baraka, Amiri, 31, 42 - 44, 59 – 61, 75, 120

Baraka, Ras J., 105, 119 - 121, 154, 166, 178, 180

Barringer High School, 75

Batons (The), 7 – 10, 22, 39

Bergen Street, 4, 31, 33, 120

Best, Earl "Street Doctor," 154

Biden, Joe, 166

Black Panther Party, 51, 75

Black Power, 23, 37, 40, 71

Bloomberg, Mike, 163

Blow, Kurtis, 77

Blue, Daniel, 17

Bontempo, Michael, 93, 94

Booker, Cory, 157, 159, 160 – 167, 170, 176 – 178

Bostic Jr., Floyd, 6, 8, 9, 13, 24, 25, 44, 70, 182

Brando, Marlon, 21

Braswell, Horace, 6, 7, 9, 13, 151

Braswell, Paul, 120

Bridge Club, 28, 87

Bronze Shields Headquarters, 86, 87, 115, 116, 151, 156

Brown, Raymond "Ray," 26, 27

Campisi Crime Family, 79

Carlin, Leo, 11, 14, 23, 24

Carroll, Diahann, 21

Carroll, Sally, 38, 39

Index

Carter, Jimmy, 82

Car theft (Stolen car), 100, 102, 103, 109

Celester, William, 104, 123, 159

Chaney, James, 22

Chicago, 48, 57, 166

Civilian Review Board, 28

City National Bank, 89, 90

Sr. Clara Muhammad School, 77

Clinton, Hillary, 166

Clinton Place Junior High School, 44

Club Mentors, 91

Cocaine, 101

Coleman, Claude, 14, 16, 72, 75, 99, 124

Coley, Sheilah, 112 – 116, 128, 129, 152, 175 – 177, 179, 180

Columbians (police organization), 10

Committee for Unified Newark (C-FUN), 44

Community Relations Bureau/Department, 100

Congress of Racial Equality, 38

Consent decree,

    (1972 Bronze Shields lawsuit), 116

    (ACLU investigation) 174

Cottle, Bobie, 13, 37, 44

Crack (narcotic), 101

Crips and Bloods (gangs), 167

Crown Heights Affair, 76

Daniels, Dannette "Strawberry," 116 – 119, 117, 178

DeMaio, Samuel, 174, 176, 179

Department of Civil Service (New Jersey), 53 - 56

Index

Du Bose, James, 74, 181

Earl Harris, 93, 94, 97

Emeralds (police organization), 10

Emergency Response Team (E.R.T.), 119

Equal Employment Opportunity Commission (E.E.O.C.), 125

Essex County, 7, 22, 94

Evens, Alonzo, 150, 181

Falcons (police organization), 10

4th Precinct, 12, 29, 31, 38, 39, 166

Fraternal Order of Police (F.O.P.), 13, 87, 92, 121, 122, 125 - 127, 178, 179

Fruit of Islam, 78

Garner, James, 21

Gentrification, 163, 182

George, Barbara, 106, 112, 114, 128, 176

Gibson, Harold, 16, 24, 26, 41, 43, 51, 52, 72, 76, 95

Gibson, Kenneth A., 23 - 25, 42 - 44, 48, 51, 52, 61, 64, 66, 71, 72. 82, 83, 93, 97, 142, 183

Glover, Ronald, 150, 152 - 154, 157, 158, 165

Goodman, Andrew, 22

Greenleaf, Louis, 72, 99, 100

Hamm Lawrence "Larry," 154

Hawthorne Avenue, 102

Hedgespeth, Thomas, 22

Hispanic Law Enforcement Society, 144

Holmes II, Levi A., 150, 154, 155 - 157, 159, 178

Houston, Whitney, 77

Howard, Frank, 14, 16, 99

Hudson Bank, 90

Human Rights Commission, 38

Index

Imperiale, Anthony, 33, 46, 59 – 61

Internal Affairs, 58, 117, 170, 172 – 174, 181

Jackson, Jesse, 21, 43, 48

James, Sharpe, 25, 45, 93, 96 – 103, 121 – 124, 127, 128, 157, 159 – 164, 166, 177

Jones, Lamont Russell, 104

Karenga, Maulana, 59

Kawaida Towers, 59 – 63

Kerr, Anthony, 140, 153

Kerr, Edward, 63, 64, 66, 67, 74

King Jr., Martin Luther, 18, 21, 38, 87

King, Rodney, 120

Knox, Charles "Pop," 14, 41, 44, 67, 72, 101

Larkins, Calvin, 61, 87, 88, 98

Leaks, Bobby, 117, 118, 122

March on Washington, 17 – 21

Martial Arts, 78

Maysey, Tasha, 104

Mattison, Jackie, 159

McCarthy, Garry, 158, 163 – 166, 169, 170, 173

Melvin, Walter, 175

Minor, Clifford, 14, 16, 162

Mississippi, 22

Moments (The), 76

Mosque #25, 73 – 75, 77 – 80

Muhammad, Elijah, 78, 79

Mustafa, Shakoor, 119, 122 – 126

National Association for the Advancement of Colored People (NAACP), 15, 38, 39, 148, 157, 165

National Guard, 20, 32, 33

Nation of Islam, 73, 75, 77, 78, 105

Index

Newark Housing Authority, 87

Newark Police Department (NPD), 5, 6, 13, 14, 18, 37, 53, 67, 68, 70, 71, 73, 93, 100, 104, 107, 108, 116, 122, 128, 141, 148, 163, 165, 170 – 174

Newark Riots (1967 rebellion), 3, 27 - 34, 44, 116, 142

New Jersey Baptist Convention, 38

New Jersey Devils, 158

New Jersey Performing Arts Center (NJPAC), 159, 163

New World of Islam, 78 – 80

New York Giants, 76, 77

Nixon, Richard, 82

Non-profit organization, (a 501c3), 155, 178

North Ward, 3, 4, 33, 46, 59, 60, 79

N.W.A, 120

Ohio Players (The), 76

Osborne Terrace, 102

Quintana, Luis, 177, 179, 180

Parker, Paul, 9

Pendergrass, Teddy, 76

People's Organization for Progress, 154

Personnel Investigation Department, 58

Prudential Center, 159

Ramadan (Muslim Holy Month), 115

Redden, John, 49 – 51, 59, 61 – 63

Roberts, Anthony, 175

Rankin, Robert, 164, 165

Rutgers University, 40, 54

Sexual Assault Rape Analysis unit (SARA), 128

Shabazz, James, 73, 74, 78

Sharpton, Al, 105

Index

Shomrims (police organization), 10

Schwerner, Michael, 22

Smith, Mae, 106, 109, 111, 120

Smith, John (1967 rebellion), 27, 39

Sniper, 32

South Ward, 4, 25, 29, 30, 34, 45, 93, 110, 117, 118

Spellman, Eloise, 32

Spina, Dominick A., 13, 38, 42, 47, 49, 51

Spruill, Carl, 14, 16, 24, 44, 46, 47, 49, 64, 76, 87

Steuben Society, 10

Student Nonviolent Coordinating Committee (S.N.C.C.), 15, 23, 27

Sunni Muslim, 122

Symphony Hall, 48, 85, 92, 149

Terrace Ballroom, 76, 149

Toto, Frederick, 32

United Afro-American Association (The), 38

Villani, Marie, 65

Washington, Harold, 166

Weequahic, 74, 80

West Ward, 3, 30, 35, 84

White House, 82

Williams, Edward "Eddie," 2, 38, 39, 40

Williams, Hubert, 14 – 16, 52, 67, 68, 70 – 72, 74, 83

Wonder, Stevie, 48

X, Malcolm, 127

"young turks," 14, 15, 36, 37, 51, 67, 71

zero-tolerance, 123, 163, 166 – 169,

Zizza, Charles, 39

Zoo Crew, 117, 119, 120, 178

Made in the USA
Middletown, DE
12 December 2024

66852607R00113